D0229868

PATHWAYS

TIMELINES OF THE ANCIENT WORLD

· ·

PATHWAYS

TIMELINES OF THE ANCIENT WORLD

··

Mike Corbishley

MACDONALD YOUNG BOOKS

First published in Great Britain in 1995 by
Macdonald Young Books
Campus 400
Maylands Avenue
Hemel Hempstead
Hertfordshire HP2 7EZ

All rights reserved. No part of this publication may be
reproduced, stored in a retrieval system or transmitted by any
means, electronic, mechanical, photocopying or otherwise,
without the prior permission of the publisher.

A CIP catalogue for this book is available from the
British Library

ISBN 0 7500 1600 0

Commissioning Editor: Thomas Keegan
Editor: Jill A. Laidlaw
Designer: Simon Borrough
Picture Researcher: Juliet Duff
Illustrators: Swanson Publishing Ltd., Jonathan Potter,
Robina Green, Steve Roberts,
Debbie Kindred (Simon Girling & Associates)
Adrian Barclay, Lee Montgomery (Beehive Illustration)

Text copyright © 1995 Mike Corbishley
Illustrations copyright © Macdonald Young Books

Printed and bound in Hong Kong

Cover illustration: Jonathan Potter

Map artwork
Beehive Illustration/Adrian Barclay: Pages 14–15, 24–5,
32–3, 52–3, 62–3, 72–3, 80–81. **Swanson Publishing Ltd.**:
Pages 17, 22, 27, 30, 35, 37, 39, 43, 45, 48, 51, 55, 59, 61,
65, 66, 71, 75, 83, 85, 87.

Illustrations
Beehive Illustration/Lee Montgomery: Page 16 top left,
centre; 17 bottom; 26 bottom; 28 centre; 38 centre; 39
bottom; 41 centre; 43 bottom; 50 top left; 51 centre; 54
bottom left; 55 bottom left; 65 bottom right; 66 bottom left; all
illustration on page 74; 78 top left; 84 bottom right. **Steve
Roberts**: Page 21 centre, right and bottom right; 22 left,
bottom centre and right; 29 bottom centre and right; 31 top
right; 35 bottom right; 43 bottom right; all illustration on page
42; 45 centre; 54 right; 58 left ;59 bottom left, bottom centre;
all illustration on page 60; 70 centre, bottom right, left; 75
bottom left; 77 bottom right; 84 centre right. **Robina Green**:
all illustrations on pages 68–70. **Deborah Kindred**: Page 16
right; 27 top left; 29 top left; 31 top left; 38 bottom centre; 40
bottom right; all illustration on page 44; 46 centre, top left; 49
top centre; all illustration on pages 56–7; all illustration on
page 67; 82 bottom left, bottom right; 83 top left, bottom
centre; 85 top, centre, bottom left. **Jonathan Potter**: Page 16
centre; 22 centre; 31 right; 37 bottom; 40 bottom; 49 bottom;
58 bottom; 64 bottom; all illustration on page 76; 78 bottom;
80 centre; 84 left; 86 bottom.

Picture Acknowledgements
The author and publisher would like to acknowledge, with
thanks, the following photographic sources:

Michael Holford: 19 centre, 26, 27, 29, 35,46 bottom, 50,
54,56 **Ancient Art & Architecture Collection**: 19 left, 31, 34,
36 left, 38, 40, 41, 46 above,49, 59 left, 79. **Werner Forman
Archive**: 23, 48, 59 right, 83. **Ronald Sheridan**: 36 right.
C. M. Dixon: 65. **Robert Harding**: 67 left, 67 right.
The Bridgeman Art Library: 38 right, 61. **The Mansell
Collection**: 87.

CONTENTS

Words in **bold** are explained in the glossary on pages 88–90.

TimeLines

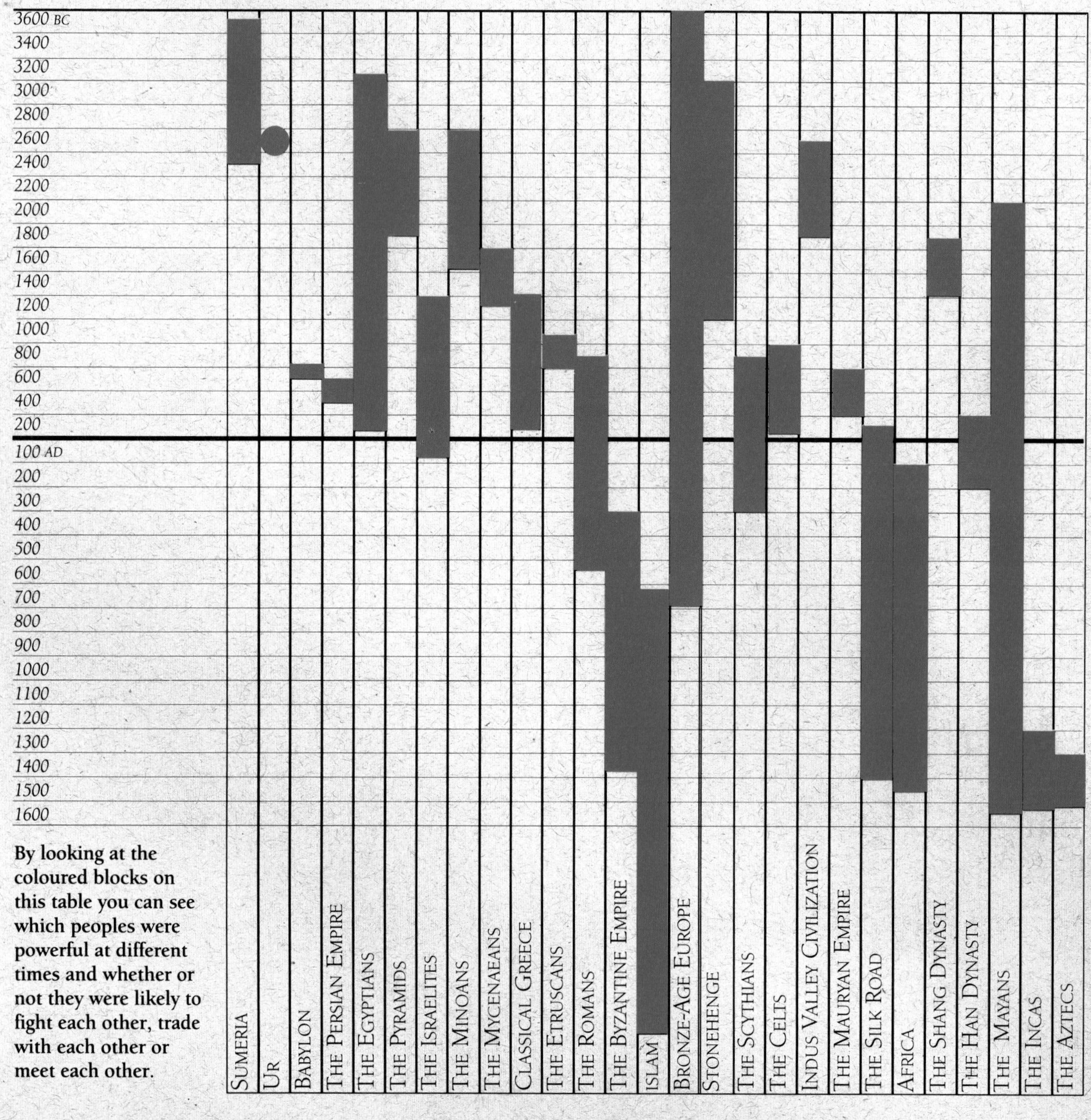

	3600 BC	3400	3200	3000	2800	2600	2400	2200	2000	1800	1600	1400	1200	1000	800	600	400	200

By looking at the coloured blocks on this table you can see which peoples were powerful at different times and whether or not they were likely to fight each other, trade with each other or meet each other.

SUMERIA
UR
BABYLON
THE PERSIAN EMPIRE
THE EGYPTIANS
THE PYRAMIDS
THE ISRAELITES
THE MINOANS
THE MYCENAEANS
CLASSICAL GREECE
THE ETRUSCANS
THE ROMANS
THE BYZANTINE EMPIRE
ISLAM
BRONZE-AGE EUROPE
STONEHENGE
THE SCYTHIANS
THE CELTS
INDUS VALLEY CIVILIZATION
THE MAURYAN EMPIRE
THE SILK ROAD
AFRICA
THE SHANG DYNASTY
THE HAN DYNASTY
THE MAYANS
THE INCAS
THE AZTECS

100 AD
200
300
400
500
600
700
800
900
1000
1100
1200
1300
1400
1500
1600

INTRODUCTION

Today it is possible to travel thousands of kilometres by air from one continent to another in just a few hours. The world seems like a small place because images of people from far-off countries are beamed into our front rooms on to our television sets. In ancient times, travel was difficult and slow — many parts of the world would have been far too dangerous for strangers. Even today, people without modern technology, such as jet travel and television, often know little about the lands and the peoples beyond their own countries or even beyond their own villages.

Despite these difficulties, there were connections between ancient peoples thousands of years ago. *Pathways* tells the stories of some of those connections. This book does not cover all peoples from all over the world. We have chosen the most important examples from each continent, from the earliest civilizations of the Near East to those peoples destroyed by the Europeans who first journeyed to the lands of the Americas.

THE NEAR EAST

This book starts with the world's earliest civilization, Sumeria, which was in the Near East. Sumeria was famous for a number of important inventions such as writing and the wheel, and it was also where the world's first real cities were built. We call this area the Fertile Crescent. New ideas often travelled between peoples along trade routes and, all through this book, you will find examples of those trade links between civilizations.

EGYPT AND THE BIBLE LANDS

The first ever recorded sea voyage was made from Egypt around 3200 BC. Egyptian hieroglyphs give us the details of this adventure. The chapter on Egypt and the Bible Lands shows that the ancient Egyptians did not like travelling themselves yet their merchants journeyed into Africa and across the Mediterranean.

NORTHERN EUROPE

Some important peoples — for example the Celts and the Scythians — lived in Northern Europe. The north Europeans had well-developed trade links with other peoples in their world and they built great stone monuments such as Stonehenge.

THE MEDITERRANEAN WORLD

In this chapter you will explore some of the world's most important civilizations. Greece and Rome have influenced many countries both ancient and modern.

INDIA AND AFRICA

The Silk Road, the world's longest trade route, linked China and beyond to western Europe. This chapter lets you see the links between three continents.

CHINA

Some of the world's most complex and wealthiest societies developed in China. During some periods of China's history, communication with other parts of the world was banned. At other times the Chinese looked abroad for trade and made voyages of exploration themselves.

THE AMERICAS

The final chapter of this book is about some of the world's most recent civilizations the Mayans, Aztecs and Incas. Their story ends with the coming of the Europeans to the 'New World'.

SUMERIA

BC

c. 9000 Wheat crops
cultivated in Syria
Sheep domesticated in
Mesopotamia
c. 7000 Çatal Hüyük founded
c. 6000 Farming established in
Mesopotamia
c. 4500 Boats with sails in use in
Mesopotamia

THE WORLD

BC

c. 8500 First rock art in the Sahara
region
First cultivation of wild
grasses in Peru
c. 8300 Glaciers retreat in Europe
c. 7000 First crops cultivated in
Mexico and in New Guinea
c. 6500 Britain separates from
Europe

Dates are given in the usual way — BC and AD. AD is an abbreviation of two **Latin** words *Anno Domini*. Latin was the language used by the Romans. These two words mean 'in the year of the lord'. This was the system of dating invented by the Christians. Dates are counted from the birth of Jesus Christ. This system of dating is used in most parts of the world today. For example, the first astronauts to step on to the surface of the moon did so in July AD 1969 — but this date is usually just written as 1969. Dates before the birth of Christ are counted backwards and have the letters BC after them. For example, the Roman general, Julius Caesar, first invaded Britain in 55 BC and then in the following year, 54 BC.

Sometimes we do not know precise dates for something that happened a long time ago. You will see the letter c. used before dates like these. It is also an abbreviation of a Latin word, *circa*, which means 'about'.

THE WHEAT WE EAT
*Eleven thousand years ago, **hunter-gatherer** people discovered how to tame wild animals and **cultivate** crops. These crops, called emmer and einkorn, are the wild ancestors of the wheat we eat today. These crops were first cultivated in the area known as the Fertile Crescent, which were the lands between the Zagros Mountains of Iran and southern Israel and Jordan.*

HUNTERS AND FARMERS
*The hunters of the Fertile Crescent herded **gazelles** and wild goats. Gradually they began to tame (domesticate) the goats and breed them for food. Other animals, such as sheep, became farm animals in Mesopotamia around 9000 BC, pigs around 7000 BC in Turkey, and cattle around 6000 BC in northern Africa and the lands around the Aegean Sea.*

THE PERSIANS
King Darius I (c. 522–486 BC) reorganized the territory of the Persians and by around 500 BC he controlled the largest empire the world had ever seen. Darius began building a new capital city, called Persepolis. See pages 22-23

ÇATAL HÜYÜK
Çatal Hüyük, in Turkey, was one of the largest farming villages in the Near East. By about 7000 BC, wheat and barley were being grown and pigs bred as farm animals. By about 6000 BC Çatal Hüyük was a town with a population of around 6,000 people.

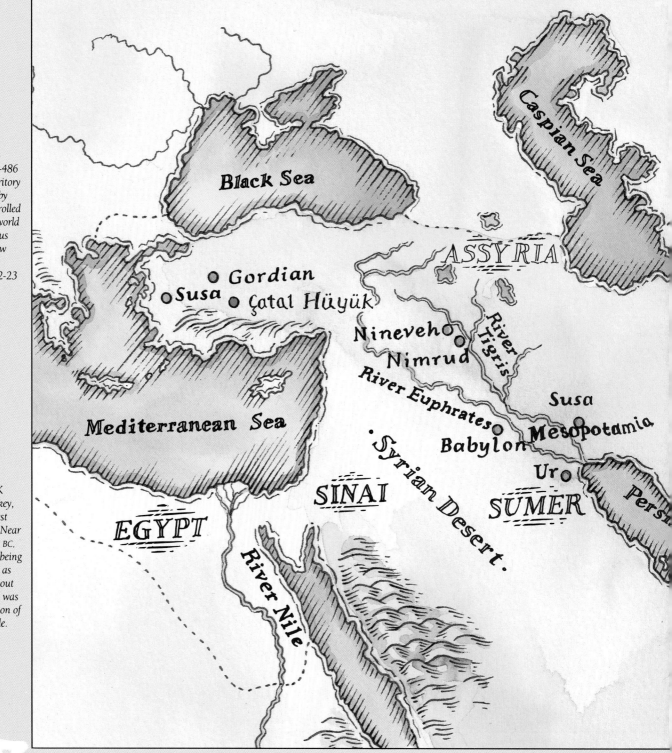

WRITING WITH PICTURES
Around 3200 BC the Sumerian people invented writing in the form of pictures. Each little drawing represented something — usually trading goods or possessions. See page 17.

WRITING ON WET CLAY
Sumerian pictogram writing developed into the writing we call cuneiform. Cuneiform means 'wedge-shaped writing'. Clerks used pens made of reed to push the wedge shapes into wet clay to form individual words. See page 17.

THE HANGING GARDENS OF BABYLON
One of the **Seven Wonders of the Ancient World** was the Hanging Gardens of Babylon. These beautiful terraced gardens, built like the architecture of a ziggurat, were said to have been built by King Nebuchanrezzar (king of Babylon from 60 BC) for his wife Amityia, to remind her of the cool green mountain area she had come from. See page 20.

GOLD AND SILVER
Persian rulers and nobles were extremely wealthy. They employed craftworkers to make beautiful objects. Turn to page 22 to see a Persian drinking horn from the fifth century BC.

CHAPTER 1:
THE NEAR EAST

It was in the Near East that some of the most important developments in the history of the world took place. People began to farm for the first time, villages grew into towns, and highly-organized societies, called civilizations, developed. In the area known as Mesopotamia, between the Tigris and Euphrates rivers, the civilizations of Sumeria, Babylon and Persia flourished. Connections were made between these civilizations — mainly through trade — and with people and countries far away.

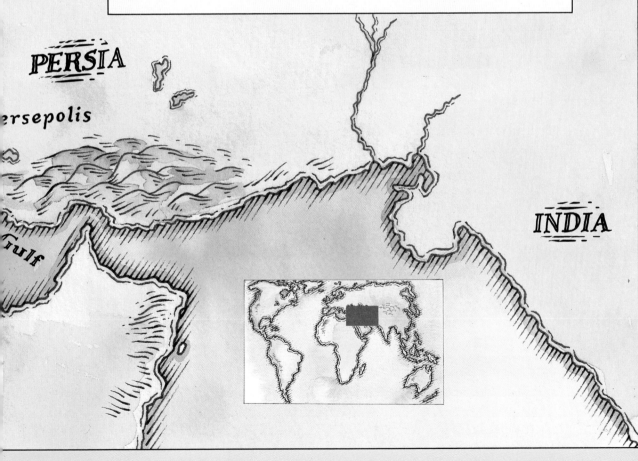

THE ISHTAR GATE
The huge city of Babylon was surrounded by walls and great gateways. Each gate was **dedicated** to one of their gods. Turn to page 21 to see a reconstruction of the Ishtar Gate, dedicated to the Babylonian goddess of love, Ishtar.

ASSYRIA
With their great armies, the **Assyrian** kings took over the kingdom of Ur in Babylonia, conquered Egypt, and controlled the eastern part of the Mediterranean Sea. The Assyrian capitals Nimrud and Nineveh were destroyed in 612 BC

ZIGGURATS
One important feature of Sumerian cities was the ziggurat — a temple tower. Ziggurats sometimes stood inside a walled **sacred** enclosure in the centre of the city. See page 19 for the Ziggurat built for the moon god Nanna in the city of Ur.

THE HITTITES
The Hittites were another of the peoples who tried to dominate the Near East. Over a period of 400 years they created an empire that even challenged the power of the Egyptians. Their powerful armies used horses and chariots. Their capital was at a place now called Bogazköy in modern-day Turkey.

SUMERIA

The world's first cities were built around 5,000 years ago in the country now called Iraq. This was the land of Sumeria (also called Mesopotamia). The land was very **fertile** and most of the people who lived in the cities were farmers. The first farming villages in the region were in northern Sumeria. By about 5500 BC wealthy farming communities were building villages which later became small towns further south nearer the Persian Gulf.

Sumeria was very organized. From the records and buildings that have been **excavated** we can identify priests, rulers, craftworkers, traders and **administrators**.

TRADE

As the Sumerians became better farmers they found that they had more food than they needed. They could trade their extra crops and **import** goods which they were unable to grow or make themselves. The rivers and the sea became major highways. The ship above is a typical Mesopotamian trading boat.

There were two harbours inside the walls of the capital city of Ur so that traders could reach the sea by the River Euphrates. The goods the traders of Sumeria imported included gold from Egypt, lapis lazuli (a bright, blue stone used in jewellery making) from Afghanistan, tin from around the Caspian Sea, timber from the coast of the Mediterranean and copper from India.

HOUSES

Buildings in towns and villages were made of timber and mud-brick. Wet soil was pressed into square, wooden brick-moulds and dried in the sun. If you were rich enough to own a house in a city like Ur, it would have been two storeys high and built around a little open courtyard (above). This design ensured that people were protected from the heat of the sun and that light could reach all the rooms.

AGRICULTURE

In northern Sumeria, farmers could rely on plenty of rain to help them grow their crops (above) and feed their animals. But in the south, where the first large cities were built, there was not enough rain for farming. The Sumerians had to **irrigate** their fields by digging canals to carry water from the spring flooding of the Tigris and Euphrates rivers.

BC
- c. 8500 First rock art in the Sahara region
  First cultivation of wild grasses in Peru
- c. 8300 Glaciers retreat in Europe
- c. 7000 First crops cultivated in Mexico and in New Guinea
- c. 6500 Britain separates from Europe

THEIR LEGACIES

The people of Sumeria were the first to organize their society on a grand scale and to build large cities. They were also responsible for a number of important inventions. The earliest evidence for the wheel comes from Sumeria. The Sumerians invented writing (cuneiform) and a mathematical system based on the number 60. They divided the hour into 60 minutes and the circle into 360 degrees. By observing the moon they worked out the lunar calendar that we still use today.

- c. 6000 First farming villages in China
- c. 4500 Farming around the River Ganges in India
- c. 3500 Simple ploughs first used in northern and western Europe
- c. 3000 Egyptian hieroglyphic writing

UR

The city of Ur (above) is famous for its excavated royal tombs and palaces. The city began to be important around 2500 BC when it had a population of around 20,000 people.

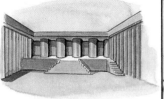

URUK

Mesopotamia was made up of independent states, called city-states. Each city-states' boundaries were based on the land around a city. One of the most important states was Uruk which was built on a river that ran into the River Euphrates. Uruk grew until its walls ran around 450 **hectares** of land and it had a population of about 50,000 people. In the centre of this great city was a sacred complex of temples. The Cone Mosaic Court above was part of this complex.

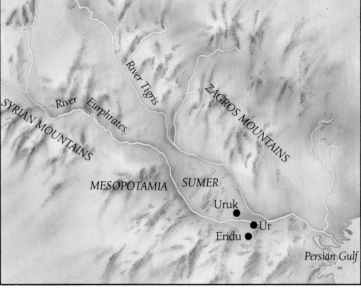

ERIDU

Eridu (above) was the most southerly city of Sumeria and probably the oldest — beginning around 5000 BC. It grew into a large and important city. **Archaeologists** have excavated two palaces of the kings of Uruk and a ziggurat (see following two pages). The city of Eridu became less important as Ur became more powerful.

WRITING

The earliest Sumerian writing looked like pictures of the goods or property that people wanted to keep a record of. These images are called pictograms. Sumerian pictograms were developed into a form of writing called cuneiform. To write in cuneiform you had to press a wedge into wet clay and then bake the clay. Each pictogram became a symbol.

Bird	Ox	Date palm	Well	Fish

BC
c. 3500 First cities in Ur
c. 2500 City-states such as Ur
in Sumeria
Royal graves in Ur —
Queen Shub-ad buried
with 74 poisoned
attendants and huge
numbers of precious objects

THE CITY OF UR

2100   Ur-Nammu rules
in Ur
c. 2000 Sumeria is invaded
by Amorites and the
dynasty at Ur comes
to an end

Ur was originally a small settlement in southern Sumeria around 4500 BC. The settlement grew into a city and its most important period began around 2100 BC under King Ur-Nammu. He ordered a defensive wall to be constructed around the city. The city was also defended by water — the River Euphrates ran along one side of the city and a canal was dug around the remaining city limits. Two harbours provided protection and docks for the ships of the city's traders.

Towering above the city, visible to everyone, was the temple tower, called a ziggurat. It was built to provide a temple to the Sumerian moon god, called Nanna. In the centre of the city were royal palaces and the tombs of previous kings. In this Royal mausoleum the kings and queens of Ur, and their servants, were buried. The houses, shops and workshops of Ur's inhabitants filled the city walls and spread out far beyond into the suburbs.

THE WORLD

THEIR ACHIEVEMENTS

The greatest achievement of the people of Sumeria was to establish a society based on cities. Very large numbers of people could be fed by the food grown on the fertile land of Mesopotamia. Not everyone had to be a farmer because food was plentiful. Other workers exchanged their labour or the products they made for food.

This head came from a marble statue. It is thought to be King Sargon who took control of the city-states of Sumeria and ruled the region as one country from around 2300 BC. His capital, Agade, has not yet been discovered.

This beautifully decorated object is a sounding box for a musical instrument. It was found in a royal tomb. This side of the box shows scenes of the king in battle with his soldiers, chariots and prisoners of war. The other side of the box shows the king at a banquet.

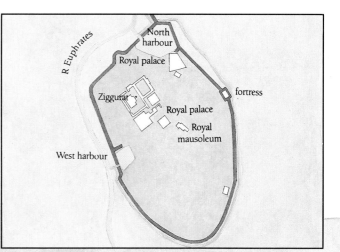

You can see a plan of the city of Ur above and a reconstruction of the city below.

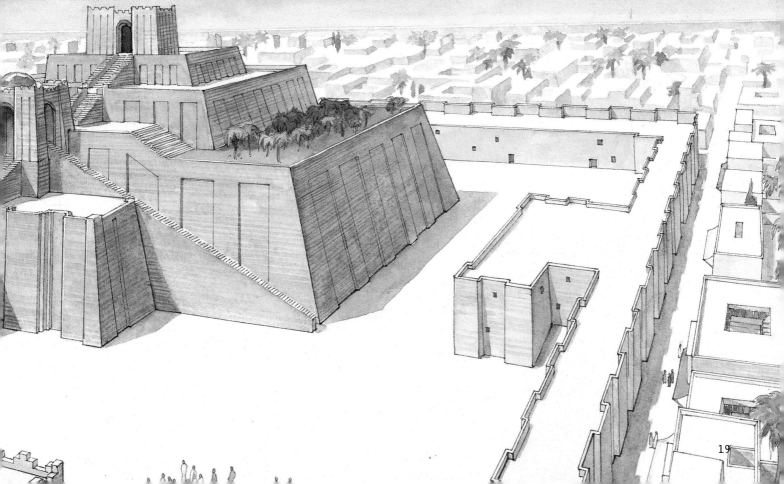

19

BABYLON

BC
2340	King Sargon I ruled from city of Agade
2330	City-states around Agade united by King Sargon
2150	Agade invaded by people of Iran
c. 2050	Warfare between Sumerian states
c. 2000	Amorite dynasties rule Babylonia

1800	Assyrians invade northern Babylonia
	Assyria established as an empire
1792–1750	King Hammurabi rules Babylon
625–539	New Babylonian Empire established
604–562	Reign of Nebuchanrezzar II rebuilds and enlarges Babylon

The Assyrian Empire (c. 1200 BC) flourished long after cities like Ur controlled Mesopotamia. This empire later fell to other powerful peoples. King Nabopolassar defeated the Assyrians and established a new Babylonian Empire in 625 BC. His son, Nebuchadrezzar, controlled a huge empire which stretched from the Persian Gulf to the Mediterranean Sea. He even fought off an invasion by the Egyptians (see pages 26–9).

King Nebuchanrezzar rebuilt the capital city, Babylon, putting up huge public buildings, temples, ziggurats and a palace. The city was defended by a canal linked to the River Euphrates which ran through the city. Defensive walls were built around the city with nine impressive gateways. But, in 539 BC, Babylon was captured by King Cyrus of Persia. A new civilization had come to Mesopotamia.

The Hanging Gardens of Babylon seemed marvellous to the travellers who came to the city. These terraced gardens brought greenery and water into a hot and dusty city.

This is a reconstruction of the city of Babylon. You can see the great ziggurat in the centre and the River Euphrates running in front of the city.

THE WORLD

THEIR ACHIEVEMENTS

The Babylonians used the Sumerians' inventions and developed their sciences of astronomy, mathematics and medicine even further. They watched the heavens carefully and were able to make accurate predictions about the year based on the movements of the sun and the moon. In the Babylonian city of Kish, the records which have been discovered of the movements of the planet Venus are so accurate that we can work out precise dates for the early kings of Mesopotamia by matching them with modern astronomical records.

King Hammurabi (1792–1750 BC) founded the first capital of Babylonia at Babylon. It replaced the original Mesopotamian capital of Ur. Hammurabi was famous for making nearly 300 laws for his people. One of the most famous laws said: *'If a citizen has put out a citizen's eye, they shall put out his eye. If a citizen has broken a citizen's bone, they shall break his bone.'* The same idea of justice can be seen in the *Old Testament* of the *Bible* (see page 31) in the phrase, *'an eye for an eye, a tooth for a tooth'.*

GOVERNING AN EMPIRE

Another of Hammurabi's laws said: *'If a citizen hired an ox and caused its death through carelessness or through beating, he shall replace an ox with an ox for the owner'.*

The kings of Mesopotamia used stones to mark the limits of their territory (below). Boundary stones were also used to record grants of land to owners.

The Ishtar Gate (below) was decorated with blue and gold bricks.

BC
539	Babylonia conquered by the Persian king, Cyrus II
522	Darius I rules the Persian Empire
500	Ionian Greeks revolt against Persian rule
492	Persians invade northern Greece
486	Xerxes succeeds his father Darius as Persian king

PERSIA

485–2	Xerxes puts down revolts in Egypt and Babylon
479	Persian fleet defeated by Greeks at Salamis
334	Alexander the Great campaigns against the Persians
330	Alexander captures the Persian capital, Persepolis

Great civilizations and empires occupied the land of Sumeria, Assyria and Babylonia. To the east were a number of **nomadic** peoples who had travelled west from Central Asia. Two of these peoples, the Medes and the Persians, were united under the Persian king Cyrus the Great. He began to conquer many lands to create an empire and, in 539 BC, captured the city of Babylon itself.

The next Persian king, Darius I, reorganized the empire and made new conquests. He fought with the Greeks (see pages 34–41) and by around 500 BC he controlled the largest empire the world had ever seen. Darius set up areas, called *satrapies*, which were governed by Persians loyal to him. A reconstruction of a satrapy governor's house can be seen below.

Persian rulers and nobles were extremely wealthy. They employed craftworkers to make beautiful objects like this drinking horn.

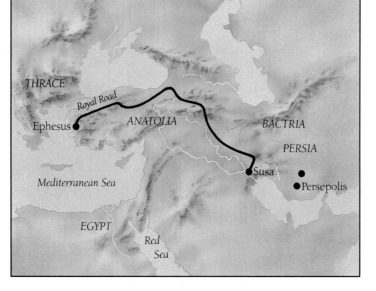

EPHESUS
Ephesus, on the western edge of the Persian Empire, was a major city standing at one end of the Royal Road. The road, which started at Susa, was constructed so that royal **couriers** could travel quickly from one end of the empire to the other. A courier could travel the 2700 kilometres of the Royal Road in a week.

THRACE
Royal Road
Ephesus
ANATOLIA
BACTRIA
PERSIA
Susa
Persepolis
Mediterranean Sea
EGYPT
Red Sea

PERSEPOLIS
King Darius decided to build a palace worthy of the greatness of his empire. He chose a site 480 kilometres south-east of Susa at a place to be known as Persepolis. Building began in about 520 BC and was not finished for 60 years, long after Darius' death. Skilled workers came from all over the empire. Some of the best stonemasons probably travelled from Greece.

BC

509	Last Etruscan king, Tarquin the Proud, expelled by the Romans
c. 500	Cast iron first used in China
	Wet rice cultivated in Japan
	Villages of hunters and fishers in Alaska
490	Greeks revolt against Persians and defeat them at the Battle of Marathon

THEIR ACHIEVEMENTS

The king of the Persians, Darius I, knew how to rule and control his huge territory. The idea of building an efficient road system was something many other emperors and dictators copied later. Darius knew that he needed to have detailed information about his empire if he was going to control it properly. He had a **survey** *carried out of all the land in the empire to decide what taxes people could afford to pay.*

447	Parthenon begun in Athens
c. 400	Olmec civilization in decline in Mesoamerica
390	Celts sack city of Rome
379	Chinese philosopher Confucius dies
c. 370	Nazca peoples settle in villages in Peru
327	Alexander the Great begins campaigns in India

A stairway in Persepolis built during the time of Xerxes I in the first half of the fifth century BC.

THE RIVER NILE

The farming land of ancient Egypt was 'the gift of the Nile' according to the Greek historian, **Herodotus**. The Egyptians called their country the 'Black Land' because each year the River Nile flooded and carried black mud on to the surrounding fields. The silt made the land very fertile and it could support crops, animals and birds.

BOATS ON THE NILE

The boat was the most important form of transport and the Nile was Egypt's main highway. The earliest Egyptian boats were made of bundles of papyrus stalks tied together. These boats were propelled by paddles or poles. Sea-going ships were given grand names such as Star of Memphis. Egyptian boats sailed from the Nile to the Red Sea, over the Mediterranean and to Nubia.

THE BIBLE

In the land of Israel the Hebrews worshipped one god, whom they called Yahweh. The sacred book of this religion and their history was in fact a collection of books which became known as the Old Testament of the Bible. It is from the Bible that we have evidence of the 12 tribes of Israel.
See page 31.

SOLOMON'S TEMPLE

The Israelite king, Solomon (966–926 BC), built a splendid temple to Yahweh in Jerusalem. The most sacred object of the Hebrew religion (later known as Judaism) — the Ark of the Covenant — was kept in the Temple.
See page 31.

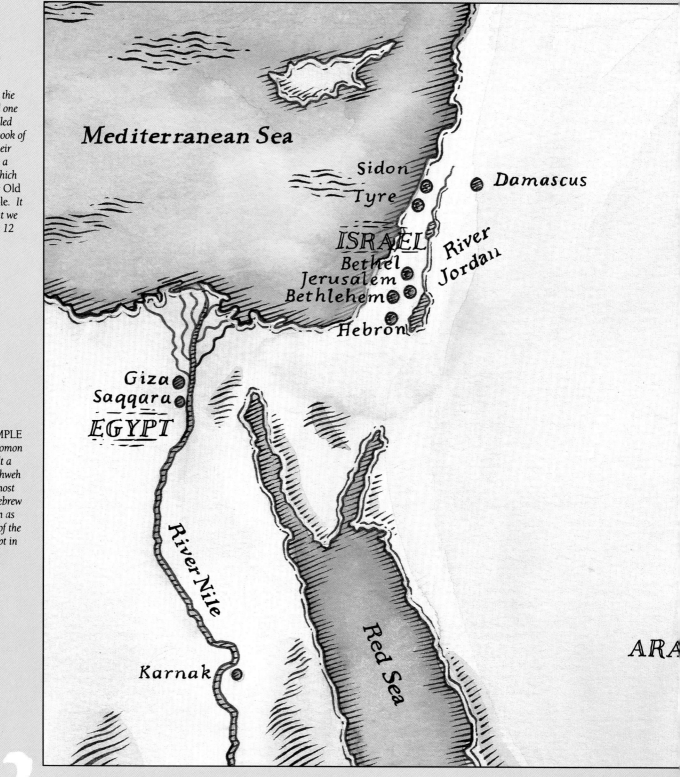

Mediterranean Sea

Sidon
Tyre
Damascus
ISRAEL
Bethel
Jerusalem
Bethlehem
River Jordan
Hebron

Giza
Saqqara
EGYPT

River Nile

Karnak

Red Sea

ARA

PEOPLE FROM THE SEA

The Egyptians wrote about enemies who 'came out of the sea'. We do not know where these sea peoples came from but they launched attacks on Egypt and other countries. Some settled as **mercenary** soldiers in Egypt, others, known as the Peleset, gave their name to the land of Palestine.

THE PHOENICIAN ALPHABET

By 1000 BC the Phoenicians developed their own alphabet which was made up of only 22 letters. The Greeks expanded this alphabet by adding vowels. The Romans then adapted the Greek version of the alphabet and this alphabet is the basis of the one we use today.

EGYPTIAN MUMMIES
The Egyptians believed in life after death and preserved the bodies of the dead to help them live for ever. Experts prepared the body for mummification in a process which often took 70 days (see page 29). Bodies were wrapped and put inside elaborately carved and painted coffins.

SACRED ANIMALS
The Egyptians kept pet monkeys and gazelles, but some animals were thought to be sacred. They worshipped the cat goddess, Bastet, and held a special festival once a year in her honour. Cats were also mummified when they died — as were several other animals. Mummified dogs, snakes, birds and fish have been found.

CHAPTER 2: EGYPT AND THE BIBLE LANDS

One of the most important civilizations in the ancient world was created by the Egyptians. They became wealthy and very powerful and influenced many peoples. The ancient Egyptians were responsible for some of the world's most extraordinary buildings — the pyramids. This chapter also looks at some of the peoples of the eastern coasts of the Mediterranean Sea who began to establish their own civilizations around 1000 BC.

KING TUTANKHAMUN
One of the most famous archaeological discoveries ever made was the tomb of King Tutankhamun (c. 1361–1339 BC). The tomb was undisturbed by tomb robbers and was discovered in 1922. The king had been buried with rooms full of marvellous objects such as model boats, boxes, board games, food and jewellery. These objects give us a detailed picture of life in the royal court around 1340 BC. See page 27.

PAPYRUS
The ancient Egyptians invented a sort of paper which continued to be used even in Roman times (after 30 BC). It was made from the stalk of a river plant called the papyrus. Read page 26 to discover how papyrus paper was made.

Persian Gulf

A

THE PHOENICIANS
Around 1200 BC people called the Phoenicians began to take over the sea trade of the eastern Mediterranean. They were great sea-faring traders and warriors. The Phoenicians established their own cities and, in Roman times, became known as the Carthaginians because their biggest city was Carthage, in north Africa.

EGYPTIAN WRITING
The Egyptians invented their own form of writing which we call hieroglyphic. Like cuneiform (see page 17), hieroglyphs were made up from pictograms. There were also signs for numbers. See page 26.

EGYPT

BC
c. 4000 Larger farming villages in
        Egypt
        Boats with sails in use on
        the River Nile
3050   Foundation of the Egyptian
        state
        First pharaoh is called
        Narmer

c. 3000 Egyptian hieroglyphics
2920   Menes becomes the first
        pharaoh of a unified Egypt
        Trade with Mesopotamia
c. 2630 First pyramid begun
c. 2600 First 'true' pyramid begun
c. 2550 Great Pyramid built at Giza

The first people who lived in the valley of the River Nile hunted and fished for food. Each year the Nile flooded and washed a layer of mud on to the surrounding land. This mud was full of **nutrients** which fed the land, which in turn fed crops and animals. Hunters became farmers because the land was so fertile.

The wealthy kingdom of Egypt thrived between 3100 and 332 BC. Egypt was originally divided into two parts — Lower Egypt and Upper Egypt. Each part was governed by one king. But in about 2920 BC the whole of Egypt became one kingdom, with a single king. Much later this king took the grand title of Pharaoh, which meant 'The Great House'. The pharaoh ruled his people with absolute power, as if he were a god. But the pharaoh needed thousands of people to help him run the country. These officials, called **civil servants**, organized big building projects, collected taxes and kept records.

The Egyptians did not rule a very large empire, but their wealth and trading connections meant that other nations owed **allegiance** to the pharaoh. Eventually Egypt was invaded by the Persians, Greeks and Romans, but many aspects of Egyptian life were adopted by these invading peoples.

This model of a boat was found in a rich man's tomb. It dates from 1800 BC.

TRADE

Egyptians did not think much of other countries. They preferred not to travel abroad but their merchants traded with many countries. The Egyptians grew plenty of barley and wheat which could be **exported**. They exchanged their grain for other goods. The land of Nubia, to the south of the kingdom, attracted the Egyptians because there were gold reserves there, as well as precious stones. A very hard black wood, called ebony, was also brought back from Nubia and used for carving ornaments and furniture. Ivory, from elephants' tusks, was a favourite material for carving. Animals such as monkeys and panthers were also imported from Nubia.

The main Egyptian trade route was the River Nile. Beyond river transport, donkeys carried goods, but camels were hardly used until Roman times. There were different types of boats — from heavy grain barges to sailing boats. Wood from cedar trees grown in the Lebanon was often used to construct the boats.

HIEROGLYPHICS

The Egyptians invented hieroglyphics — writing made up of pictograms. Pictures, some of which you can see below, were painted on to papyrus with a brush and ink or carved into stone. The Egyptians probably used about 700 hieroglyphs.

The Egyptians invented their own 'paper' to write on. The papyrus plant is a reed which grows along the banks of the Nile. The Egyptians removed the **pith** and cut the stem into strips. They laid these strips on top of each other (each layer at right angles to the one below) and beat them flat. The papyrus was left to dry and smoothed flat.

2150	Collapse of Old Kingdom
2040	Middle Kingdom period
	Egypt reunited and ruled from Thebes
	Trade with Syria and Palestine
1652	War between Egypt and Hyksos peoples from Asia
1550	Hyksos peoples driven out of Egypt
1367	New king adopts the name Akhenaten

THEIR ACHIEVEMENTS

The Egyptians became very skilful at surveying and measuring. These skills were needed for great building projects such as the pyramids and for the annual measurement of the Nile floods. A Nilometer was invented and set up on Philae island in Upper Egypt to measure the level of the water. A survey was carried out each year to establish who owned which plots of land. Greek and Roman writers tell us that the Egyptians invented the science of geometry to help them with this work.

1367	New capital of Egypt at Amarna
1339	King Tutankhamun buried
1070	New Kingdom of Egypt ends
671	Assyria conquers Egypt
285	First lighthouse in the world built at Alexandria in Egypt
31	Cleopatra, Queen of Egypt, defeated by the Romans at the Battle of Actium and commits suicide
30	Egypt becomes a Roman province

AGRICULTURE

An Egyptian hymn describes the River Nile as the *'food provider, who creates all that is good'*. The Nile was home to fish and wild game which could be caught or hunted. Huge quantities of grain could be grown after the Nile flooded the land. This photograph is of a painting on papyrus showing Egyptians ploughing and harvesting wheat and **flax** around 1346–1300 BC.

TUTANKHAMUN

The English archaeologist, Howard Carter, caused a world-wide sensation when he discovered the tomb of the boy-king Tutankhamun in the **Valley of the Kings** at Thebes in 1922. Tutankhamun's preserved body was encased in three gold coffins. The gold mask which covered his face is shown above.

SAQQARA

Saqqara was the burial place of the ancient capital of Egypt, Memphis. The Step Pyramid (above) in Saqqara was built in about 2630 BC for King Djoser.

ABU SIMBEL

Pharaoh Rameses II, who came to the throne in about 1273 BC, built two temples for himself and his wife on the island of Philae in the Upper Nile, called Abu Simbel (above).

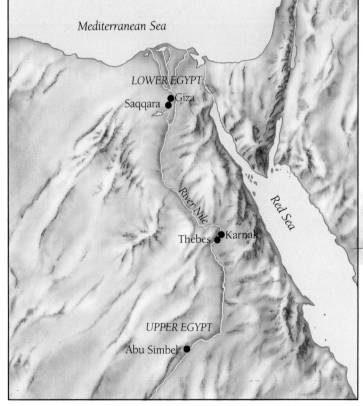

Mediterranean Sea

LOWER EGYPT

Saqqara ● ● Giza

River Nile

Red Sea

Thebes ● ● Karnak

UPPER EGYPT

Abu Simbel ●

KARNAK

In ancient times Karnak was called Thebes and it was the Egyptian capital from around 1550 BC. Several temples have been excavated there including one to the god Amun (above).

THE WORLD

BC
- c. 3200 Maize first cultivated in Mesoamerica
- c. 2500 First cities of the Indus Civilization in India
  Sahara begins to dry out
  Walled settlements in China
  Metal first used in Britain
  City-states in Mesopotamia

THEIR LEGACIES

Ancient peoples were fascinated by the Egyptians and their monuments, especially the pyramids. One of the first tourists to visit Egypt was the Greek historian, Herodotus, in the fifth century BC. He brought some of the history and the mystery of Egypt to the West. This century, the discovery of Tutankhamun brought about a new interest in Egyptian styles in architecture, decoration and furniture, which had been popular in nineteenth-century Europe. The calendar of 12 months, which was invented by the Egyptians, was introduced to the West via trade with the Romans.

- c. 2000 Inuits (Eskimos) first reach northern part of Greenland
  First settlers in New Guinea
- 1600 Shang Dynasty in China
- 1500 Mycenaean civilization established
- c. 1200 First cities in Mesoamerica
  Hittite Empire collapses

1   2   3   4   5

GODS AND GODDESSES

The sun god Amun-re (1), was shown in different forms with different names. Here (2) he is called Khepri and is shown as a **scarab beetle**. Isis (3) was the goddess of women. She was the wife of Osiris (4) and the mother of Horus (5). Horus, the sky god, is pictured as a falcon. Osiris was the god of the dead and the underworld. He was also seen as responsible for the annual Nile flood and for rebirth after death.

THE PYRAMIDS AT GIZA

At Giza in Lower Egypt was one of the Seven Wonders of the Ancient World — the pyramids. The earliest type of pyramid was the step-pyramid like the one at Saqqara (see page 27). At Giza the pyramids were constructed with smooth sides. The greatest pyramid of all, the Great Pyramid (below), was built as the burial place of King Khufu in about 2550 BC.

c. 1000 Phoenician alphabet introduced
c. 800 Maize cultivated in Mesoamerica
776 First Olympic Games in Greece
753 Traditional date for the foundation of Rome
c. 600 Phoenicians sail round Africa

THEIR ACHIEVEMENTS

Building the pyramids was a tremendous achievement for Egyptian architects, surveyors, engineers and builders. The Great Pyramid at Giza was built with 6.5 million tonnes of stone. Single stone blocks weighed anything from two to 15 tonnes each. Not only did the stones have to be brought to the building site from the quarry but each had to be cut very accurately indeed. A pyramid's sides were measured to be at an angle of exactly 52 degrees.

490 Persian invasion defeated by the Greeks
c. 300 Early Mayan period begins
221 China united by First Emperor Ch'in Shi-huang-ti
214 Great Wall of China begun
55 First Roman invasion of Britain

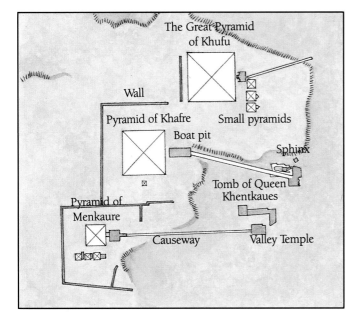

A plan of the pyramids at Giza (above). The pyramids at Giza as they are today (below).

THE NEXT LIFE

The Egyptians believed that people lived after death in the kingdom of the god Osiris. This kingdom was like a perfect Egypt. The Egyptians thought that everyone would still have the same type of life they had when they were alive — the pharaoh would still be king and farm workers would still cultivate the fields.

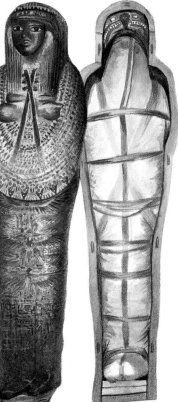

MUMMIFICATION

The Egyptians perfected the art of preserving bodies after death. This is called mummification (above). Organs like the lungs and **intestines** were removed and kept in containers called canopic jars (left). The body was then **embalmed** by packing it in a salt called natron for about 40 days. Finally, it was wrapped in bandages and put inside at least one coffin.

29

THE LAND OF ISRAEL

BC

c. 1250	Israelites living in Canaan
1020	Hebrew tribes unite
	Saul anointed king
1000	King David anointed
	Capital at Hebron
	Defeat of Philistines and kingdom expanded
	The Ark of the Covenant is brought to Jerusalem
960	David dies
960–	Solomon, David's son,
22	becomes king
	Great Temple to Yahweh built in Jerusalem

587	Jerusalem captured by the Babylonians
333	Palestine part of Alexander the Great's empire
164	Judas Maccabaeus reconquers Jerusalem from the Seleucids
63	Romans conquer Jerusalem
4	Jesus Christ born
AD	
29	Jesus Christ crucified
70	Revolt against the Romans, Jerusalem taken and Solomon's Temple burned

TYRE
Tyre was an important Phoenician settlement on the coast of Lebanon during the time of King David.

SIDON
Like Tyre, Sidon was an important trading town in Phoenicia. There is an Egyptian record which shows that 50 ships did business from Sidon alone.

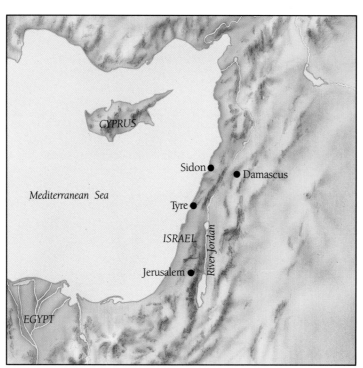

DAMASCUS
Damascus is the capital of modern-day Syria. It was noted as a trading city in Egyptian records around 330 BC. The town was conquered by the **Aramaeans** and then the Israelites but it was still an important trading city in Roman (in the first century BC) and Muslim times (in the seventh century AD).

JERUSALEM
Jerusalem was already defended by the **Jebusite** tribe when it was captured by King David around 1000 BC. Jerusalem grew even more powerful under the rule of David's son and successor, Solomon, from around 960 BC.

The Israelites were originally several different Hebrew tribes who began to move into the area shown on the map above, from around 1250 BC. About 50 years later, 12 tribes following the religion of Judaism formed a league against their enemies. The Philistines were one of their enemies who had settled in the south and gave their name to the land called Palestine. At first the Israelites had no overall king but each tribe had its own ruler. Around 1020 BC the Israelites decided to elect Saul from the tribe of Benjamin as their king. When Saul fell from favour the shepherd David was made king in around 1000 BC.

The lands of the tribes of Judah, Hebron and Israel were all united under King David. David defeated the Israelites' enemies and Israel became a great power.

BC
- c. 1200   Hittite Empire collapses
- c. 1000   Long-distance trade by peoples in Australia
- c. 800   Zapotec people produce the first writing in the Americas
- 509   Last Etruscan king thrown out of Rome
- 508   Democratic government in Athens
- c. 300   Mayan writing developed

THEIR LEGACIES

*The most important thing the Israelites left the world was their religion. Their god was called Yahweh. The Bible records an early leader, **Moses**, leading his people out of the slavery they suffered in Egypt. He also took the Ten Commandments from Yahweh which established the western custom of working for six days followed by a holy day of rest. The ideas in the Ten Commandments form a major part of the way many people behave today.*

- 214   Great Wall of China begun
- 100   North Vietnam ruled by the Chinese
- 30   Egypt made a Roman province

AD
- 24   Han Dynasty re-established in China
- 79   Vesuvius erupts, Pompeii and Herculaneum destroyed

EVIDENCE IN DOCUMENTS

We have a great deal of evidence about the people of Israel from documents — some from other peoples like the Egyptians and the Assyrians. But we also have their own writings, mainly the *Old Testament* of the *Bible*. The names of their kings and **prophets** are there for us to read.

SOLOMON'S TEMPLE

King Solomon built an elaborate temple (below) to Yahweh (God) in the capital of Jerusalem. The Ark of the Covenant was kept inside the temple. This area, the 'Holy of the Holies' was only entered once a year by the high priest. The temple was destroyed when the Romans captured Jerusalem in AD 70.

Some of the most extraordinary pieces of evidence found are the documents we call the *Dead Sea Scrolls* (above). In 1947 a shepherd stumbled across several documents in a cave in modern-day Jordan. They turned out to be the remains of the earliest hand-written books of the *Bible*, written during the life of Christ.

THE IVORY GUARDIANS

An important part of Israelite worship was the Ark of the Covenant which symbolized the presence of God in the temple. You can see the two guardians standing on either side of the chest, or Ark, which contained the laws given to Moses by God (below).

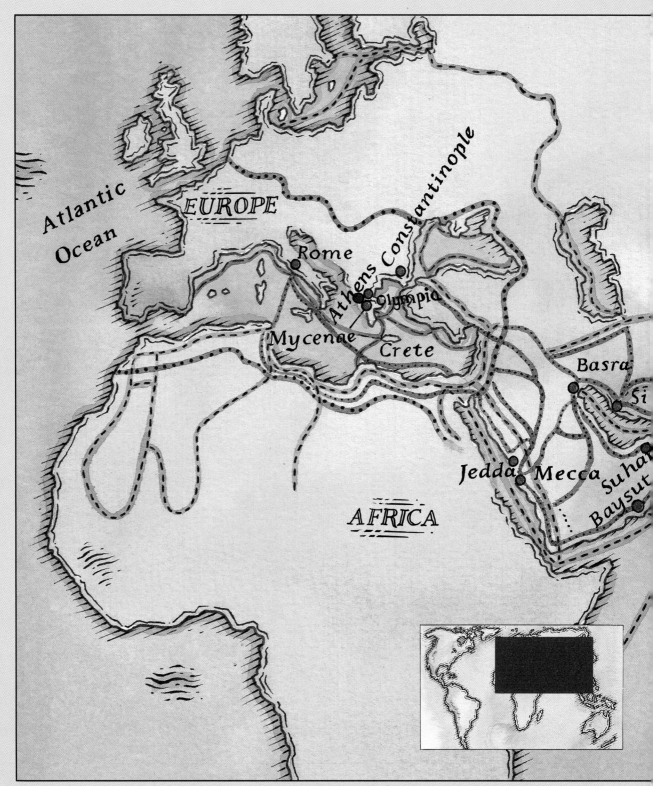

THE MONSTER OF THE LABYRINTH
*The earliest Greek civilization, that of the Minoans of Crete, gave us the myth (story) of a strange animal — the Minotaur — a bull-like creature who devoured young men and women in his **labyrinth**.*
See pages 34–5.

THE MASK OF KING AGAMEMNON
*The Mycenaeans of mainland Greece created a rich and powerful civilization and controlled the first Greek Empire. The later Greeks learnt about the Mycenaean kings and warrior heroes in the **epic** poems of **Homer** which date from the eighth century BC.*

ISLAM
A new religion called Islam was founded by the prophet Muhammad in Arabia in the seventh century AD. His followers were called Muslims and they spread their religion by conquest further east and into some of the countries around the Mediterranean Sea.
See pages 50–51.

THE BYZANTINES
*After the end of the Roman Empire the Byzantine Empire continued it in a different form in the rest of Europe. The Byzantine capital was at Constantinople (now Istanbul in Turkey). The Byzantines were Christian and established the **Greek Orthodox Church**.*
See pages 48–9.

Map labels
Atlantic Ocean
EUROPE
Rome
Athens Constantinople
Olympia
Mycenae
Crete
Basra
Si
Jedda Mecca
Suha
Baysut
AFRICA

ROMAN ENTERTAINMENT
*Most Roman towns had an **amphitheatre** where games were held and gladiators fought to the death. Live animal hunts took place in amphitheatres and criminals were often tied up to be killed by wild beasts like lions and tigers. See page 46.*

ROMAN ROADS
The first roads built in a new area conquered by the Romans were built by the soldiers. After that the roads became the responsibility of the local government. Roman roads were usually straight in sections for long distances. See page 44.

THE ACROPOLIS
You can still see the most impressive remains of the ancient Greek civilization in modern Athens. The Acropolis was the religious centre of the capital city. The most important building on the Acropolis is the temple to the city's goddess, Athena, which is called the Parthenon. See page 40.

THE OLYMPIC GAMES
Most people in the world have heard of the Olympic Games. The original Olympic Games were held in 776 BC, at Olympia in Greece, in honour of the king of the gods, Zeus. There were all sorts of sports, such as javelin and discus throwing, wrestling and chariot racing. See page 38.

CHAPTER 3: THE MEDITERRANEAN WORLD

The ancient peoples of the Mediterranean were responsible for many of the cultures which exist today in Europe and in the Middle East. Four groups of peoples had the biggest influence on the ancient and modern world — the Greeks, the Romans, the Byzantines and the Muslims. The ancient Greeks gave the world democracy. The Romans carved out a great empire whose boundaries we can still see today. The Byzantine religion is still strong in countries as far apart as Greece and Russia, while Islam is also the religion of millions of people throughout the world.

GREEK ARCHITECTURE
Skilful Greek architects designed and constructed various styles of architecture. You can still see Greek styles of architecture in many parts of the world used in modern buildings. See page 41.

THE ETRUSCANS
The Etruscans were a powerful people who originally lived north of Rome. Many of their inventions and beliefs were taken over by the later Romans. See pages 42–3.

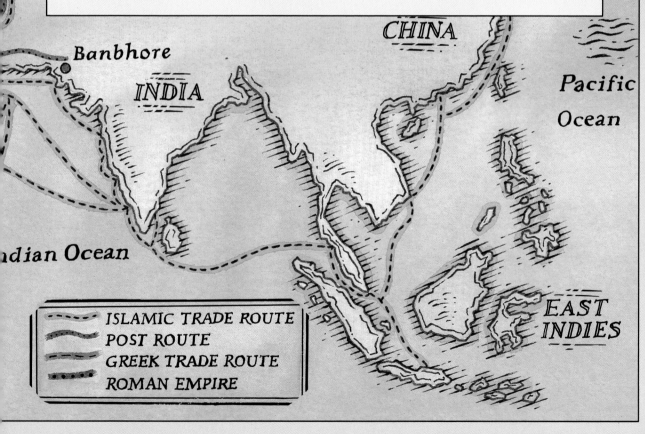

CHINA

Banbhore

INDIA

Pacific Ocean

Indian Ocean

EAST INDIES

- --- ISLAMIC TRADE ROUTE
- ≈≈ POST ROUTE
- — GREEK TRADE ROUTE
- •••• ROMAN EMPIRE

ROMANS AT WAR
The Romans conquered a huge empire which had 60 million people living in it by the second century AD. They needed a large and well organized army to conquer and control their new lands. See page 46.

ROMAN GOVERNMENT
Roman citizens voted for all of their government officials, generals and judges. Their parliament was called the senate. Then, in the first century BC, emperors appointed themselves to govern. See page 44.

THE MINOANS

Many wall paintings have survived from Knossos. This one shows the sport of bull-leaping. One acrobat grasps the bull's horns and is tossed over the animal's back. Notice that the figures are similar to those in Egyptian paintings (see pages 26–9) because Minoan artists were influenced by Egyptian art.

Crete is a large island in the Mediterranean Sea between mainland Greece and Egypt. The Egyptians called the island of Crete 'the land of the Keftiu' and they traded there regularly. The people of ancient Crete are usually called Minoans, after their legendary king, **Minos**. Around 4,000 years ago Crete was a wealthy trading nation. The island's rulers built huge palaces, like the one at Knossos (below). Their palaces had many rooms with corridors and balconies built around an open courtyard. We know that the Minoans worshipped gods such as the Earth Mother and the God of Beasts — you can still see bulls' horns decorating their buildings.

For hundreds of years there were a great many people living in ancient Crete — in towns as well as in palaces. But around 1450 BC life came to a sudden end when buildings were destroyed by a massive volcanic eruption on the island of Thera 130 kilometres away.

An artist's impression of the palace centre of Knossos (below). Knossos as it is today (opposite page).

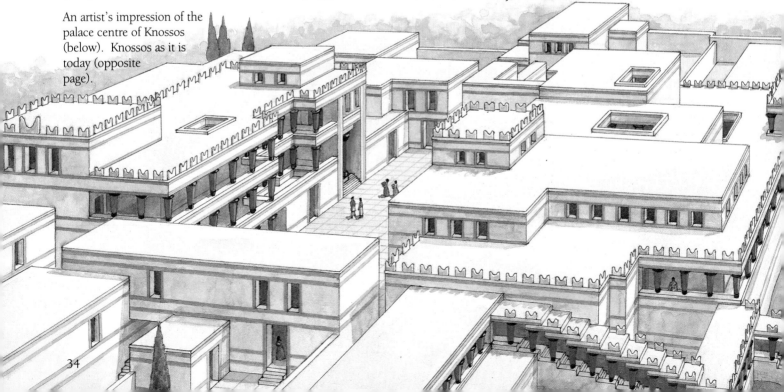

THE WORLD

BC
c. 2500 City-states, such as Ur, in
Mesopotamia
First cities established in the
Indus Valley
Sahara begins to dry out
c. 2000 Earliest pottery made in the
Andes region of South
America
First settlers in New Guinea
c. 1550 New Kingdom in Egypt

THEIR ACHIEVEMENTS

*The Minoans established a wealthy civilization which stretched far beyond the island of Crete. They invented a form of writing, which is known today as Linear A. Linear A has not yet been **deciphered**. During their own times the Minoans were known for the quality of their pottery and clothes. They were good metalworkers and produced beautiful gold jewellery.*

c. 1400 First written inscriptions in
China
c. 1200 Beginning of the Olmec
civilization in Mesoamerica
1000 David anointed King of
Israel
c. 500 First Chinese 'coins' used
270 Asoka becomes ruler of the
Mauryan Empire in India

GOURNIA

Gournia (above) was the site of both a palace and a busy harbour town. Its houses were built on the steep slopes that rise up from the sea. The townspeople became rich through trade, metalworking, fishing, weaving and farming.

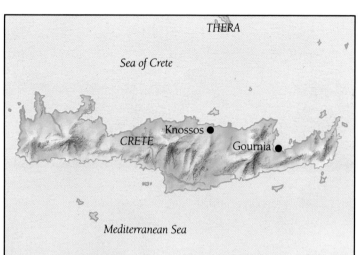

KNOSSOS

Knossos must have been the king's palace. There is a Greek legend that says that King Minos kept a creature, half-bull and half-man, called the Minotaur, in a maze under the palace. Each year seven boys and seven girls were sent from mainland Greece to be sacrificed to the creature.

TRADE

The Minoans travelled all over the Mediterranean as traders but also settled on islands like Thera and Kythera. Merchant ships from Crete exported wine, olive oil and luxury items such as painted pottery. Examples of Minoan pottery have been found in countries on the eastern Mediterranean coast. We know that the Minoans also traded with Egypt and took gifts to the pharaohs of Egypt.

Food such as olive oil, wine or grain was stored in huge pottery jars . Palaces had store-rooms full of these jars. Potters usually decorated their work. This jug for water or wine is decorated with a seaweed pattern.

THE MYCENAEANS

BC
c. 2000	Mycenaean people first appear in Greece
c. 1600	Small Mycenaean kingdoms develop
c. 1500	Mycenaean kingdoms become very powerful on mainland Greece and on neighbouring islands
1450	Volcanic eruption on island of Thera — Minoan civilization destroyed

	Mycenaeans occupy and govern Crete
1250	Mycenaean army attacks the city of Troy
c. 1200	Mycenaean kingdoms under threat. Strong defences are built around their settlements
c. 1150	Mycenaean cities gradually abandoned. Mycenae destroyed

No one knows why the Minoan civilization collapsed — some archaelogists think that a volcanic eruption on the island of Thera (a Minoan **colony**) destroyed the culture, and others think that the Minoans were wiped out by a massive tidal wave. After the collapse of the Minoan civilization on Crete, the island was occupied by the Mycenaeans, who were named after their home town of Mycenae on mainland Greece. The Mycenaeans were a warlike people who had already established a number of small kingdoms in Greece. By about 1500 BC they were the most powerful people in Greece.

They went to war with the eastern Mediterranean and attacked the city of Troy. Troy, now called Hissarlik in modern-day Turkey, was well known to the later Greeks through Homer's poem, *The Iliad*. *The Iliad* tells the story of how the King of Mycenae, Agamemnon, led an army of Greeks to **besiege** Troy. After a long siege, the Greeks tricked the Trojans into opening their gates by leaving a great wooden horse outside as a gift and then pretending to sail away. The Trojans dragged the horse inside their walls. The horse was full of Greek soldiers who let in the rest of the army and destroyed the city.

AGAMEMNON

In 1876 a German archaeologist, Heinrich Schliemann, excavated this gold **death mask** from Mycenae (left). He believed that it was the face of King Agamemnon himself. The mask was found with a number of other treasures such as daggers, gold cups, necklaces, rings and swords.

THE LION GATE

This is the grand entrance to Mycenae itself (below). Lions were a symbol of the power of a king. Notice the walls and the gateway itself. These walls, made out of huge blocks of stone, were called Cyclopaean by the later Greeks, who thought that the legendary giant **Cyclops** must have built them.

THE TOMB OF ATREUS

Mycenaean kings were buried in huge underground tombs built in the shape of a beehive (right). The body was placed in a central vault together with weapons and precious goods. This one, at Mycenae, is said to be the tomb of Atreus, the father of the famous Greek warrior Agamemnon.

THE WORLD

THEIR ACHIEVEMENTS

*The name Mycenae, and the name of its king, Agamemnon, were known to every child in ancient Greece. The stories of the war with Troy, as told by the poet Homer, were part of the history of Greece. It was from Mycenae that Agamemnon started on the Trojan expedition. It was at Troy that the Greek hero **Achilles** killed the Trojan champion, Hector.*

The Mycenaeans controlled the first Greek empire with strongholds, like Mycenae, at Tiryns, Nauplion, Thebes and Athens.

TIRYNS

The city of Tiryns (above) was constructed on a rocky hilltop as a Mycenaean stronghold. It was built to be difficult to get into with thick walls, several gates and high-walled corridors.

GREECE
Gulf of Corinth
Thebes
Aegean Sea
Athens
Ionian Sea
Mycenae
Tiryns
Mirtoan Sea
CRETE

MYCENAE

Mycenae (below) was a hill-top town, well defended by strong outer walls. There were houses built inside and outside the walls. The palace of the king was built on a high and rocky point in the centre. It had its own terraces, staircases and rooms built around a high hall.

CLASSICAL GREECE

BC
c. 1000	Mainland Greeks begin to emigrate to Asia Minor
c. 900	Greeks trade with the Near East
776	First Olympic Games held
c. 750	Greek colonies established in Sicily and southern Italy
c. 550	Sparta, on the Greek Peloponnese, is the most powerful city-state
508	Democratic government in Athens
490	Invading Persians defeated at the Battle of Marathon
480– 79	Persians invade Greece Athens raided, the Acropolis is destroyed

No one knows what happened in Greece after the collapse of the Mycenaean Empire. Around 1200 BC a new group of people, called the Dorians, moved into central and southern Greece. The Dorians spoke a **dialect** of Greek. Greece does not have much land which can be farmed easily. One hundred years after the end of the Mycenaean Empire the people of mainland Greece began to **emigrate** to more fertile lands. Colonies were set up on the coasts of Italy, France and Spain, in north Africa and in Asia Minor (on the coast of present-day Turkey and around the Black Sea).

At first this new Greek empire was divided into a number of small states based on cities — called city-states. From about 700 BC the Greek states became wealthier, mostly because of trade. They often fought for control of more land. Two of the most powerful city-states were Athens and Sparta who fought each other in the Peloponnesian War from 431 to 404 BC.

Sometimes the Greeks were threatened by enemies from outside — for example the Persians (see pages 22–3) tried to occupy Greece on several occasions but were always defeated.

LANGUAGE

The word alphabet comes from the names of the first two Greek letters — alpha and beta. The Greeks took their alphabet from the Phoenicians — and called the letters *phoinikeia*, which means 'Phoenician things' in Greek. The Greeks added their own letters to the Phoenician alphabet (below).

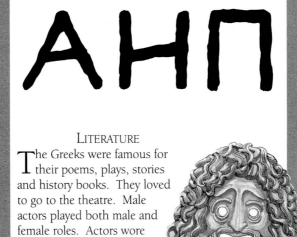

SPORT

The Greeks held festivals for their gods. Some of these festivals included sporting competitions. The most important one was held at Olympia in honour of the king of the gods, Zeus. The first Olympic Games were held in 776 BC. The photograph above is of a plate (from the fourth century BC) showing two athletes competing in the discus and javelin.

LITERATURE

The Greeks were famous for their poems, plays, stories and history books. They loved to go to the theatre. Male actors played both male and female roles. Actors wore masks to show what sort of character they were playing.

WAR

Greek soldiers wore heavy body armour and carried a spear and a sword. This vase shows the hero Achilles killing an enemy

HOMER

We think that Homer's poems were composed around 800 BC. Apart from *The Iliad*, he also created *The Odyssey*. This was the story of the hero **Odysseus** returning to this home on the island of Ithaca after the Trojan War.

480	Persian fleet defeated at the Battle of Salamis				334	Alexander the Great's campaign against the Persians	
479	Persian army defeated at the Battle of Plataea				333	Alexander defeats the Persians at the Battle of Issus	
447	Parthenon begun in Athens				86	Romans capture Athens	
431–404	War between Athens and Sparta. Spartans victorious						
358	Macedonia, in northern Greece, unified under King Philip II						

THEIR LEGACIES

The ancient Greeks were great artists. Greek sculptors made statues, in stone and bronze, of their gods and famous people, such as writers, politicians and generals. Their art has made it possible for us to see what the ancient Greeks really looked like and what they wore.

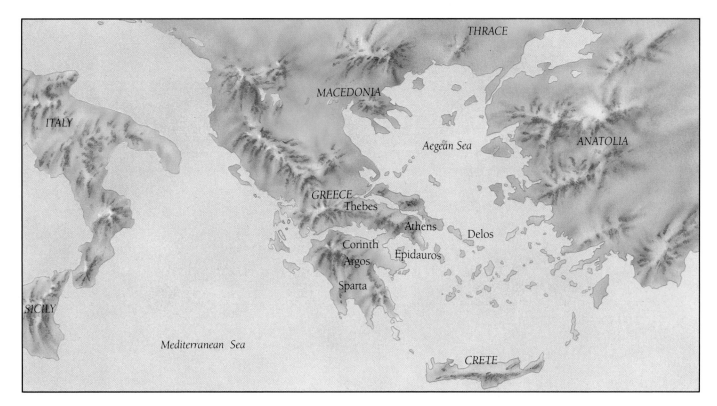

EPIDAUROS

The theatre at Epidauros was just one of the special buildings erected for the god of medicine, Asklepios. Epidauros is the best-preserved ancient Greek theatre. The acoustics are so good that you can hear the smallest noise on stage from the highest seats.

TRADE

The Greeks were great traders. They produced large quantities of wine and olive oil — goods which were in great demand in other countries because of their high quality. The Greeks also exported their painted pots in huge numbers. In exchange, Greek merchants brought back grain, timber, salted fish and purple dye. Some Greeks travelled as far as Britain, India and Africa.

COINS

The first Greek coins were used by the merchants of Aegina, an island near Athens. Around 560 BC the merchants began to make coins out of silver with a turtle design on them which was the symbol of their city. The owl was the symbol of Athens.

ATHENS

By the fifth century BC Athens (above) had become the capital of a great empire. The Athenians depended on their strong navy for protection and on their merchant ships for trade so they enlarged their port at Piraeus and joined it to Athens by two parallel walls.

Many Greek towns had an acropolis. The word acropolis means the 'high city' and it was usually the best-defended place in the city. In Athens during Mycenaean times the Acropolis (see below) was a fortress which contained the king's palace. Later, the Acropolis became a religious centre filled with temples to the gods and goddesses.

In 476 BC a new Acropolis was planned and work began on a stronger wall to protect a larger area containing more temples. The largest temple was dedicated to the city's goddess, Athena, and was called the Parthenon. It was begun in 447 BC and took 15 years to build. Inside was a gold and ivory statue of Athena over 11 metres high.

c. 400 Olmec civilization in decline
321 Chandragupta establishes the Mauryan Empire in India

THEIR ACHIEVEMENTS

Classical Greece gave the world some of its finest literature. Many later peoples have been influenced by Greek plays and poetry. Much of this literature is still taught in schools in western Europe. Stories of Greek heroes, such as Herakles (called Hercules by the Romans) and gods, such as Zeus and Poseidon, are known to millions of people all over the world.

146 Carthage destroyed by the Romans
c. 100 Okvik hunting people settle in northern Alaska

ARCHITECTURE

The Greeks were very skilled architects, especially when building with stone and marble. Marble blocks had to be cut very carefully in the quarry and transported to the temple site where they were trimmed into their final shape. The stonemasons used no mortar (cement) to join the blocks together. The Greeks used three types of decoration on the **capitals** of the columns that held up their public buildings (right). The columns were named according to the type of decoration on the capital. Doric columns were used on the Parthenon. Ionic columns were used in eastern Greece and on some of the islands. A few temples had the Corinthian type of column which became very popular in Roman times.

Doric

Ionic

Corinthian

The Parthenon as it is today.

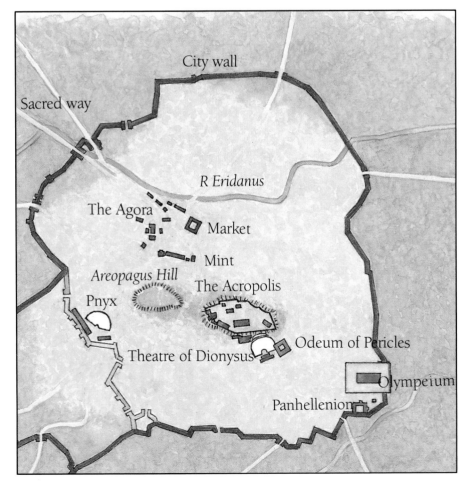

City wall

Sacred way

R Eridanus

The Agora

Market

Mint

Areopagus Hill

Pnyx

The Acropolis

Theatre of Dionysus

Odeum of Pericles

Olympeium

Panhellenion

A plan of Athens.

THE ETRUSCANS

BC
- c. 900 Etruscan peoples living in area north of Rome
- c. 800 Etruscans expand into Latium, Campania and the Po Valley
  12 separate Etruscan states
- 616– Reign of the Etruscan king
- 579 Tarquin I
- 550 Etruscan cities ruled by governors elected each year from this date

- 509 The last Etruscan king of Rome expelled — called Tarquin the Proud by the Romans
- 474 Etruscans defeated in a naval battle at Cumae by the Carthaginians
- 413 Etruscans help the Athenians besiege Syracuse
- 392 City of Veii captured by the Romans
- 100 All Etruscan cities now controlled by the Romans

The Etruscans lived north of Rome from about 900 BC. By the seventh century BC the Etruscans had formed 12 separate states. These city-states were independent but **allied** to each other. The people who lived in each of the city-states had a similar way of life, supported each other and communicated with each other.

The Etruscans were very rich people. Their wealth came from farming, trade and industries such as metalworking and pottery. Gradually they wanted to control more land. They conquered other peoples in the north of Italy as far as Mantua and in the south as far as the Bay of Naples.

TRADE

The Etruscans traded with the Greeks, the Phoenicians and the Egyptians. This ostrich egg (above) was made into a container for liquids. It was brought from Egypt by the Etruscans and then painted in a style copied from Greek pottery.

WAR

We can see Etruscan armour and weapons in this small bronze statue made in the fifth century BC. It was used as a religious offering and probably shows Mars, the god of war.

This pottery jug (above) shows an animal sacrifice to the gods. This two-handled gold cup (left) was placed in the tomb of a wealthy Etruscan.

TOMBS

The Etruscans believed in life after death. Highly-decorated underground tombs were built for wealthy Etruscans. There were steps down to the chamber and a great mound above the ground. Burial chambers were built like houses for the dead, complete with furniture. The walls were decorated and objects were left for the person to use in his or her next life.

Many tomb wall paintings show Etruscan people. We know that this lady with an elaborate hair-style was called Velia because of a tomb **inscription**.

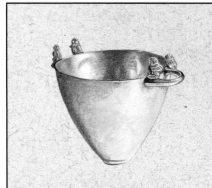

ARTISTS AND CRAFTSPEOPLE

There were many gifted and skilled metalworkers and potters in Etruscan cities. Their metal and pottery objects were prized by other peoples in the Mediterranean. They made a special type of pottery (see left) called *bucchero*. Metal objects, in gold, silver and bronze, were usually highly-decorated. The little cup (also left) has intricate figures fixed to its two handles. Unfortunately many of these Etruscan objects were stolen by treasure hunters who broke into underground tombs.

BC
- c. 900 Oldest known Olmec centre at San Lorenzo destroyed
- 814 Carthage founded as a new Phoenician city
- c. 800 Zapotec people in Mesoamerica produce the first writing in the Americas

THEIR LEGACIES

The greatest Etruscan legacy was to pass on their discoveries to the Romans. For example, the Etruscans gave the Romans the idea of gladiatorial games (see page 46). The Romans were taught how to plan their cities with streets, sewage systems and water supplies by the Etruscans. Even the name for Rome itself, Roma, was originally an Etruscan word.

- 480 The Persian king, Xerxes, attempts to conquer Greece but is defeated
- 221 Beginning of the reign of Chinese emperor Ch'in Shi-huang-ti
- 146 Rome finally destroys Carthage
- c. 100 North Vietnam ruled as a Chinese province

ROME

The last kings to rule the city of Rome before the rise of the Roman Empire were Etruscan. At that time (the early sixth century BC) Rome was a large city surrounded by a wall almost seven kilometres long. An Etruscan artist made this bronze statue (above) of the she-wolf which **suckled** the city's founders, Romulus and Remus (see page 44).

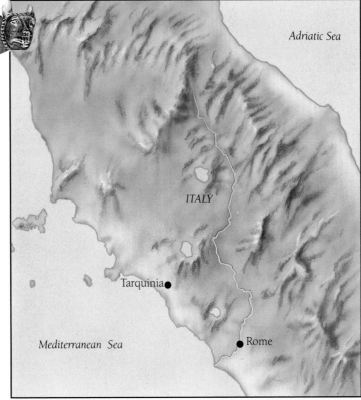

Adriatic Sea

ITALY

Tarquinia●

Mediterranean Sea

●Rome

TARQUINIA

Some decorated Etruscan tombs have been found at Tarquinia. The one above shows a feast. The painting was made in the fifth century BC.

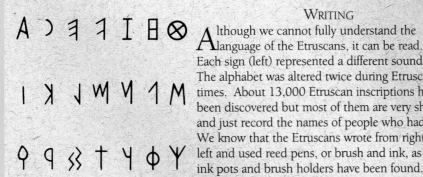

WRITING

Although we cannot fully understand the language of the Etruscans, it can be read. Each sign (left) represented a different sound. The alphabet was altered twice during Etruscan times. About 13,000 Etruscan inscriptions have been discovered but most of them are very short and just record the names of people who had died. We know that the Etruscans wrote from right to left and used reed pens, or brush and ink, as both ink pots and brush holders have been found.

You can see the whole alphabet on this little jar, which is perhaps an ink pot. It was found in a tomb.

THE ROMANS

Roman children learnt that their city had been founded by the twins, Romulus and Remus who were abandoned as babies but then rescued and suckled by a she-wolf (see page 43) and brought up by a shepherd around 753 BC.

The area around Rome was occupied by various groups of people, including the Etruscans. The Latins eventually became the most powerful group and threw out their Etruscan king, Tarquinius, in 509 BC. The people of Rome then set up a special kind of government called *res publica* which literally meant 'a matter for the people'. All the officials of the government were voted into office by the citizens of Rome. We call this a republic.

The Roman state increased in size over the years, mainly because Roman armies conquered other peoples. After 500 years of republican rule ambitious politicians began to seize power for themselves and one, called Augustus, was made Rome's first emperor in 31 BC. This time is the called the Empire Period.

The Romans needed a large army to control their empire (see map opposite) and a civil service to administer Rome's affairs. They built towns in all the lands (called provinces) they controlled.

By the sixth century AD, most of the Roman Empire was overrun by different peoples. Only the city of Constantinople (see pages 48–9) survived.

COINS

During the Republican Period Roman coins often carried the name of the official responsible for making (minting) the coin. During the Empire Period the head of the emperor was shown.

ROADS

A vast network of roads (above) were built all over the Roman Empire by conquering armies and province authorities. Many Roman roads are still used today in France and Britain.

Senators (right) discussed all important issues. The two highest officials were called consuls. The consuls were allowed to hold joint power over the government and army for one year.

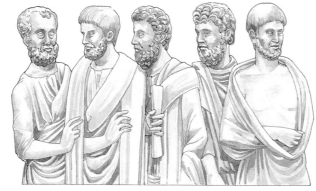

GOVERNMENT

During the Republican Period officials were voted into Rome's parliament — called the senate. Not every adult person could vote — women and slaves were excluded. The senate was made up of people who had held government posts. Under emperors like Hadrian (AD 117–38) (above), the senate still existed and officials were voted into jobs, but the emperor held the most power.

AD	
14	Emperor Augustus dies
64	Great fire in Rome
79	Vesuvius erupts. Cities of Pompeii and Herculaneum near Naples destroyed
80	Emperor Titus opens the world's largest amphitheatre in Rome, the Colosseum
122	Emperor Hadrian visits Britain. Hadrian's Wall begun

312	Christianity declared Rome's official religion
330	Emperor Constantine moves capital of Roman Empire to Constantinople (now Istanbul)
455	Rome invaded by Vandals
475	Romulus Augustulus the last Roman emperor in the West

THEIR ACHIEVEMENTS

By the time of the Emperor Hadrian in the second century AD there were probably 60 million people living within the frontiers of the Roman Empire. It was one of the biggest, and longest-lasting empires the world has ever seen. People could say 'I am a Roman' even if they were living in provinces as far apart as Britannia (Britain) or Aegyptus (Egypt). Latin was the official language of the empire but people across the Roman world also used their own languages and dialects.

EPHESUS

The remains of the city of Ephesus can still be seen in modern-day Turkey. This was the capital of the Roman province of Asia. Ephesus' theatre was rebuilt to hold 25,000 people in the first century AD.

COLCHESTER

Colchester (above) was the capital of England when the Roman Emperor Claudius invaded in AD 43.

TRADE

By the second century AD trade routes had been established all over the empire. Huge amounts of corn were imported into Rome just to feed the capital's 200,000 poor people. Goods, food, animals and slaves came into Ostia, the port of Rome, from far off countries — perfumes from Arabia, silk from China, spices from India. Wild animals were imported in huge numbers from Africa.

POMPEII

'Everything is drowned in the flames and buried in the ashes of sadness'. This is what the Roman poet Martial (AD 41–104) wrote about the destruction of Pompeii by the volcano Vesuvius, which erupted in AD 79.

Before the eruption Pompeii was a prosperous town. It had originally been an Etruscan town but became a colony for retired Roman soldiers and their families in 80 BC.

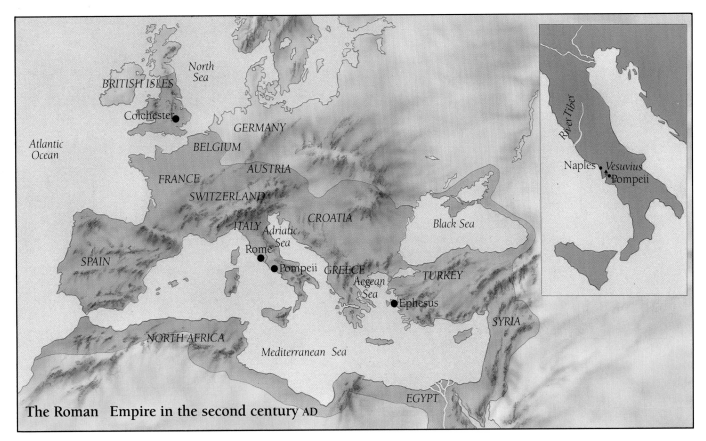

The Roman Empire in the second century AD

THE WORLD

BC
- c. 750 Greek colonies in the Mediterranean
- c. 700 Scythians move into eastern Europe from Asia
- 671 Assyrians conquer Egypt
- c. 600 Phoenicians sail around Africa

THEIR ACHIEVEMENTS

*Julius Caesar (c. 100–44 BC) wrote that the Romans 'eagerly copied any good idea, whether it was from a friend or an enemy'. The Romans were good at solving problems and at building and construction. They surveyed roads and towns using instruments to mark out right angles and level surfaces. They brought water supplies into towns by building great **aqueducts** which conveyed huge quantities of water for homes, industries and public baths. This use of aqueducts was learnt from the Etruscans.*

- c. 500 Villages of hunters and fishers in Alaska
- 479 Confucius, Chinese philosopher, dies
- c. 300 Mayan writing develops
- 214 Great Wall of China begun
- c. 185 Mauryan Empire in India in decline
- c. 100 Celts build defended settlements in Europe

THE ARMY

The Roman Empire had a professional army. About 45,000 soldiers were trained in units of about 5,600 men called a legion. Soldiers served for 20 years on average and then were entitled to a lump sum of money and a plot of land, but they had to stay 'on reserve' in case they were needed.

A Roman legionary in full armour ready for battle. He is protected by metal-plated armour on his chest and shoulders and a metal helmet. He carries a short sword, a dagger and a spear.

GODS

Religion was very important to ordinary Romans. They believed that their gods were responsible for everything that happened and that sacrifices had to be made to them to keep them friendly. Many Roman gods were originally Greek and Etruscan.

Mithras, originally the Persian god of light and truth, became a Roman god of victory (above).

THE COLOSSEUM

The Emperor Titus completed this amphitheatre, known as the Colosseum (above), in AD 80. It held 50,000 people and in the opening ceremony alone, 9,000 animals were killed in 100 days of games. Gladiators fought to the death to entertain people. The amphitheatre was named after a colossal (huge) statue of the Emperor Nero which stood nearby.

The remains of the **Forum** in Rome (right).

c. 60   Kushan Empire established
         in India
100   First use of paper in China
150   Buddhist religion reaches
         China

THEIR LEGACIES
*The Romans had a great effect on huge
numbers of people throughout their empire.
There are many examples of Roman ideas
and technology surviving in later cultures.
Their language, Latin, passed into other
European languages such as French and
Spanish. You will find many Latin words
used in English — for example, family
(which in Latin is* familia*), actor (this is
the same word in Latin) and second (which
is* secundus *in Latin).*

c. 300   Golden age of Mayan
         civilization begins
429   Vandals invade north Africa
         and establish a kingdom
c. 450   Teotihuacán the sixth-
         largest city in the world

ROME
This is a drawing of what we think Rome looked like during the Empire Period (below). The Emperor Augustus (63 BC–AD 14) set about adding new public buildings to the city. He reorganized the whole city and its entire population of about one million people.

There were villages on the seven hills which made up the area later called Rome by about 1000 BC. The first real town grew up under Etruscan rule. It grew quickly and was surrounded by a wall in the third century AD.

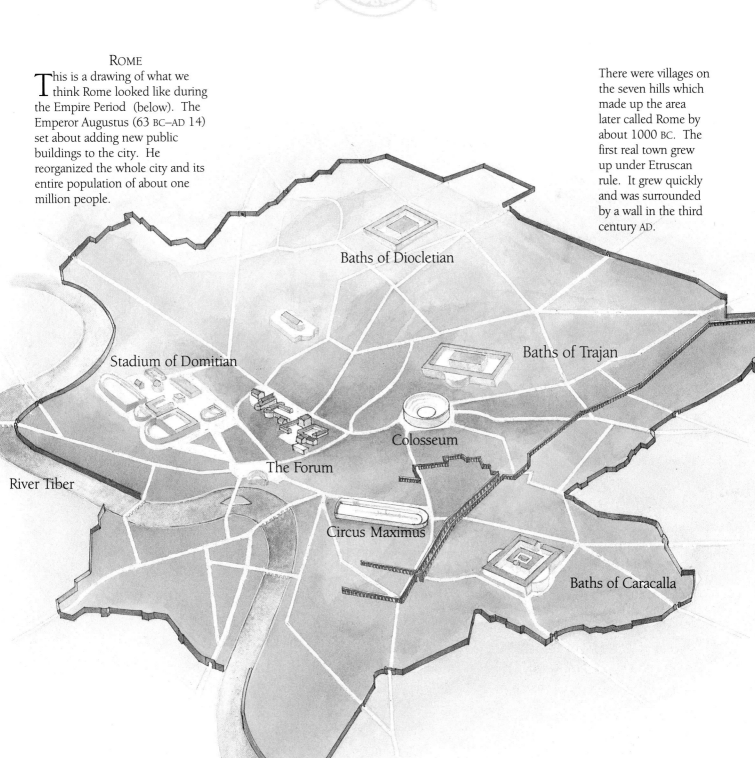

Baths of Diocletian

Baths of Trajan

Stadium of Domitian

Colosseum

The Forum

River Tiber

Circus Maximus

Baths of Caracalla

BYZANTIUM

MOSAICS

The Romans took the craft of making mosaic pictures, for floors, walls and ceilings, from the ancient Greeks. Mosaic making continued during the Byzantine period. Many mosaics, made from tiny pieces of stone, tile and glass, decorated the churches of the Byzantine Empire such as this one (above) in Venice, Italy.

The eastern Roman Empire continued to act as a major force in the world from its capital of Constantinople even after the western Roman Empire had been defeated by **Barbarian** tribes (about AD 476). The empire became known as the Byzantine Empire because Byzantium was the original Greek name for Constantinople.

The Byzantine Empire really began with the reign of Emperor Heraclius in 610. He ruled peoples who were Greek-speaking and Christian. He defeated the Persians at Nineveh in 626. The Byzantine Empire was under threat from other peoples for centuries. The Muslims (see pages 50–51) were the most serious threat in the seventh and eighth centuries. In the ninth and tenth centuries the empire flourished but was eventually overcome by the Islamic **Ottoman Turks** in the fifteenth century.

TRADE

Trade was very important to the Byzantines. Their cargo ships and overland trade routes allowed them to sell goods as far north as Britain, into eastern Europe and the Middle East as well as across the Mediterranean Sea.

CHRISTIANITY

Constantine the Great ruled Constantinople from AD 330 and was the first Christian Emperor in the world. As the Byzantine Empire grew, the church sent out **missionaries** to convert unbelievers to Christianity and to build churches. The church of San Vitale in Ravenna, Italy (above), (AD 526–547) is a typical Byzantine church.

MOUNT ATHOS

Mount Athos, in northern Greece, still has working monasteries (above) which were founded in Byzantine times. By 1321 the monasteries' lands covered 20,000 hectares.

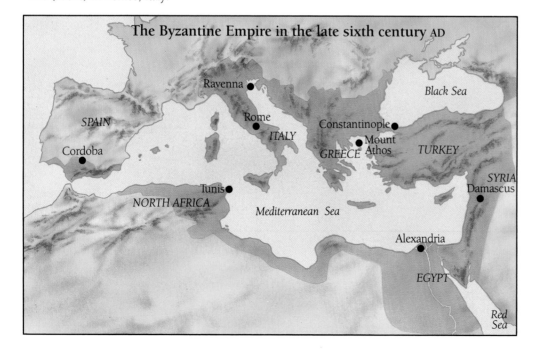

The Byzantine Empire in the late sixth century AD

SPAIN

Cordoba

Ravenna

Rome

ITALY

Tunis

NORTH AFRICA

Mediterranean Sea

Black Sea

Constantinople

Mount Athos

GREECE

TURKEY

SYRIA

Damascus

Alexandria

EGYPT

Red Sea

THEIR LEGACIES

The greatest Byzantine legacy is the Orthodox Church, which still thrives in many countries today. The Greek Orthodox Church and the Russian Orthodox Church are still well-established because of Byzantine missionaries. Byzantine art and architecture influenced later peoples in Europe. **Scholars** *in Constantinople preserved many ancient Greek and Roman books which were eventually passed on to the West in copies after the city was captured by the Turks in 1453.*

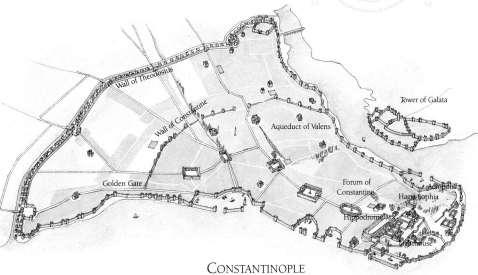

CONSTANTINOPLE

The new city's name meant the 'city of Constantine' — Constantinople (above). Its original name, Byzantium, became the name for the provinces ruled from the city. During Roman times the empire was divided into two — the capital of the west was Rome, the eastern capital was Constantinople. The original walls of the city, put up in AD 330, sealed off too small an area for the growing population. New walls were constructed by Emperor Theodosius in the fifth century.

This is the Byzantine Church of the Holy Cross in Turkey.

HAGHIA SOPHIA

The church of Haghia Sophia (left) (which means 'Holy Wisdom') was begun by the Emperor Justinian in about AD 532 and completed five years later — at that time it was the largest church building in Europe. Today it is a mosque (see page 50) in the Turkish capital, Istanbul.

ISLAM

By the sixth century, three of the world's most important religions had been founded — Christianity, Hinduism, Judaism and Buddhism. A new religion, called Islam, which was to create a new empire in the Middle East and the Mediterranean area, was founded by Muhammad in 610 in Mecca. Muhammad became a merchant and, after hearing messages from God, began to preach his religion, called Islam which means 'submitting to God'.

The Arab Muslims then began to spread their religion and empire further. They moved west into Egypt and north Africa and north and east, taking over Syria, defeating Byzantine forces, and taking over the Persian Empire. Muslim armies also occupied parts of Spain and north-west India. They even defeated a Chinese army in 751. In 1453 Muslim amies occupied Constantinople and put an end to the Byzantine Empire.

Viking ships like these (above) sailed along rivers to Russia and were carried overland to trade with the Byzantine and Islamic Empires.

NAVIGATION AND TRADE

As the Islamic Empire grew, new markets for goods were created. Each town had a *souk*, or street market. Traders from far-off lands brought their goods here to sell or exchange. Cities such as Damascus and Baghdad became rich because of trade. By 750 the Muslims controlled all the trade between the Red Sea and China.

Goods were transported by two main methods — land or sea. Merchants travelling on overland routes were well supplied by *caravanserais* — road stations providing food and shelter for **caravans**. Merchants travelled by sea in dhows to northern Europe, the Black Sea, the Far East and east Africa.

All sorts of goods were imported and exported. The Muslims produced a range of luxury goods in wood, metal, glass, tile, **ceramic** and textiles. In return, they imported slaves, gold and ivory from Africa, furs from the **Baltic** and spices and ceramics from the Far East.

Muslim astronomers imported this instrument, called an astrolabe, which was invented by the ancient Greek scientist, Hipparchus. Muslim seafarers used the astrolabe to measure their position against the position of the sun or stars. This one (above) was made in the ninth century AD.

PATTERNS

Muslim artists were forbidden by their religion to create pictures of any living creature — people or animals. Instead they used an amazing range of patterns and shapes which were carved or painted (above).

MOSQUES

All Muslim towns have buildings called mosques which are used for worship and study. Each mosque has a courtyard and a covered hall for prayer. There is also a *mihrab*, which is a niche in the wall showing the direction of Mecca. Worshippers are called to prayer at set times of day from tall towers.

THE WORLD

AD
531–79	Persian Sassanid Empire at the height of its power
560	Irish monk Columba founds a church on Iona, Scotland
606	First written examination for Chinese civil service entrants
634	Christianity spreads to Northumbria, England
736	Founding of the city of Dhillika, the first city of Delhi

THEIR LEGACIES

In some modern-day non-Islamic countries, such as Spain and Portugal, you can still see the influence of Islamic architecture and art. Throughout the centuries, Muslims have been famous for their learning and inventions. There is a ninth-century Muslim library at Cordoba, in Spain, which contains half a million books. Muslim scientists made advances in medicine, algebra and mathematics, astronomy and navigation. The counting system we use today in the West was given to us by Muslim mathematicians.

750	City of Teotihuacán destroyed by fire
c. 800	Towns develop in North America
	Bow and arrow first used
	West African kingdoms established
	Charlemagne crowned Holy Roman Emperor by the Pope

MEDINA

Muhammad met a lot of opposition to his religion in Mecca so he set up a Muslim community in Medina.

JERUSALEM

The mosque shown above is the Dome of the Rock, built by AD 699 in Jerusalem. It was from here that Muslims believe Muhammad rose up to heaven.

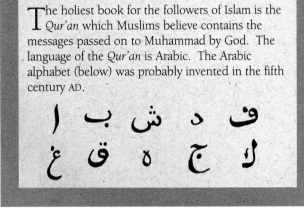

ARABIC

The holiest book for the followers of Islam is the *Qur'an* which Muslims believe contains the messages passed on to Muhammad by God. The language of the *Qur'an* is Arabic. The Arabic alphabet (below) was probably invented in the fifth century AD.

ا ب ش د ق
غ ق ه ج ك

MECCA

Mecca was a sacred place for Arabs even before Muhammad's time. Muhammad and his followers upset the rich merchants of Mecca who were worried that their wealth would disappear if people did not visit the holy shrine there.

BAGHDAD

Baghdad was founded by Arabs and was always full of foreign visitors. The caliph (ruler) built the city in a circle and by 814 it was the world's largest city.

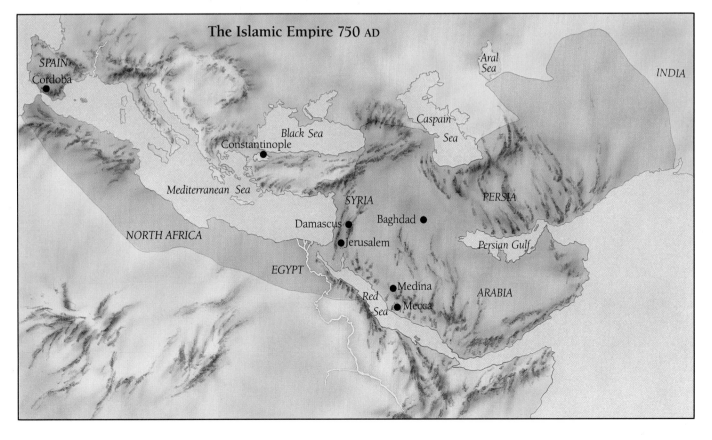

The Islamic Empire 750 AD

SPAIN
Cordoba
INDIA
Aral Sea
Caspain Sea
Black Sea
Constantinople
Mediterranean Sea
SYRIA
PERSIA
NORTH AFRICA
Damascus
Baghdad
Jerusalem
Persian Gulf
EGYPT
Red Sea
Medina
Mecca
ARABIA

MAKING BRONZE
By about 1200 BC many everyday objects used in Europe were made of bronze — weapons, tools, household utensils and jewellery. Bronze is a metal made of copper and tin. See pages 54–5.

THE MILK DRINKERS
*The Scythians were called the 'horse-milkers' and 'milk-eaters' by the Greeks because they made a drink, called koumiss, from the **fermented** milk of female horses.*

FIERCE WARRIORS
Celtic warriors were fierce. Some made themselves look frightening by painting patterns on their bodies and spiking their hair. They carried shields and fought with swords and spears, from fast-moving chariots drawn by horses. See page 60.

FROM GERMANY TO THE MEDITERRANEAN
The defended Celtic settlement of Heuneburg in southern Germany was the stronghold of a noble family who lived here around 400 BC. The style of the defences (they are like Greek strongholds) and the range of imported goods (wine, fine pottery and jewellery) from the Mediterranean that have been found here show that the family had many contacts with other countries. See page 61.

MAIDEN CASTLE
The Celtic peoples of northern Europe built defended towns to live in. This one, now called Maiden Castle, is in southern Britain. Its huge banks and ditches the — distance from the bottom of a ditch to the top of the bank was 14 metres! — must have put off many invading enemies. See page 61.

WEAPONS AND A WAGON
We know a lot about the Scythians from the tombs of their rich nobles. The wooden walls of burial chambers were brightly painted and a great number of everyday objects and weapons were placed in tombs. See page 58.

WASSERBURG
One of the defended settlements of the peoples of Bronze-Age Europe was discovered in southern Germany in the Federsee Lake. It is called Wasserburg. Around 1200 BC the settlement was made up of about 40 houses which were strongly defended by wooden walls and gates.
See page 55.

THOUSANDS OF STONES
In many parts of north-western Europe, circles and lines of stones were put up for rituals or religious ceremonies. One of the most impressive stone sites is the row of stones at Carnac in Brittany, France. Thousands of stones stretch in parallel lines across the landscape.
See page 55.

CHAPTER 4: NORTHERN EUROPE

This part of the book covers the years from about 7000 BC to the occupation of north-western Europe by the Romans in the first century BC. This was a period of prehistory for most of the people of Europe — this means that people did not use writing. It was an important time in the history of northern and central Europe because various peoples came together to form tribes, nations and countries.

STONEHENGE
Of the 900 stone circles that exist in Britain, Stonehenge is the most famous. It was probably constructed as a sort of temple for ceremonies and religious rituals.
See pages 56–7.

MOVING HUGE STONES
The builders of Stonehenge must have been clever to get the huge stones (some weighing 50 tonnes) into position.
See pages 56–7.

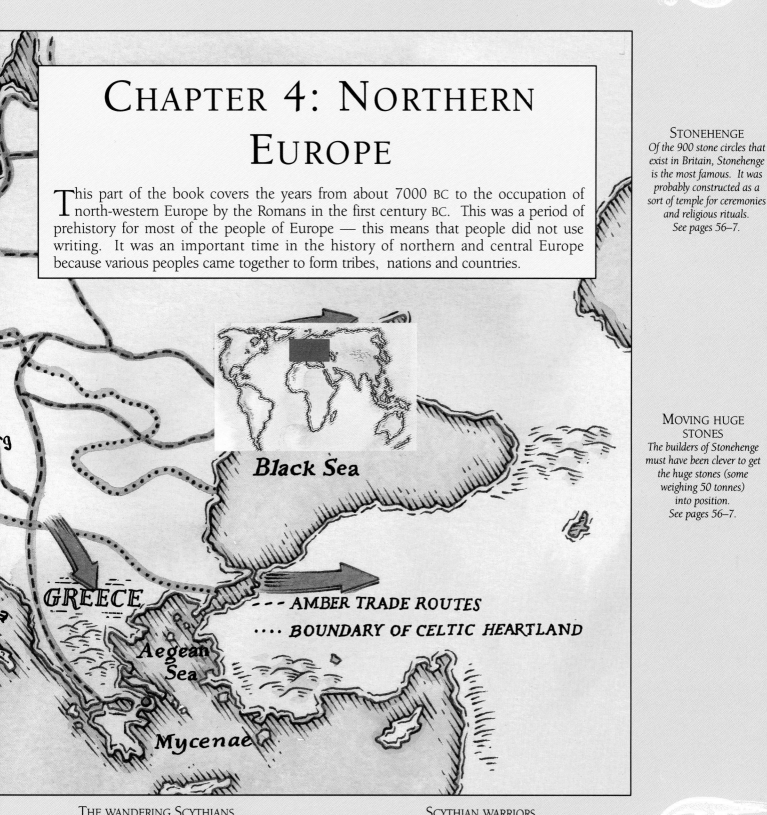

Black Sea

GREECE

- - - **AMBER TRADE ROUTES**

···· **BOUNDARY OF CELTIC HEARTLAND**

Aegean Sea

Mycenae

THE WANDERING SCYTHIANS
The Greek historian Herodotus wrote about the Scythians. He tells us that they were 'people who take their dwellings with them. Their homes are their waggons'. These waggons contained all the family's possessions and travelled about eight kilometres a day behind their herds of cattle, sheep and horses.
See pages 58–9.

SCYTHIAN WARRIORS
The Scythians were a warlike nomadic people who lived to the north of the Black and Caspian Seas. Scythian nobles rode horses into battle which were beautifully covered with reins and saddles made of brightly-coloured leather and felt.
See page 58.

53

BRONZE-AGE EUROPE

BC
- **c. 7000** Copper mined in Romania, Hungary, Yugoslavia. Gold also made into ornaments
- **c. 4000** Knowledge of metalworking passes to other parts of Europe
- **c. 2300** Bronze working spreads to Europe including Britain and northern France

- **c. 2000** Increasing number of fortified settlements in eastern and central Europe
- **c. 1250** New weapons and armour made of bronze
- **c. 1200** Most everyday objects made of bronze
- **c. 700** Iron in common use

Hunting and farming peoples needed a good supply of strong materials to make tools and weapons. At first stone, especially flint, was used. But by about 6000 BC people had discovererd that copper ore (see opposite page) could be worked into different shapes. Stone tools did not disappear overnight but metal tools gradually replaced them — bronze at first, followed later by iron. The peoples of the Bronze Age (c. 4000 BC) in Europe began to claim land and build settlements. Some were simple villages, but in central and eastern Europe they began to build **fortified** settlements. People became more warlike, perhaps because they wanted to defend their farming land — and the strongest warriors were the rulers.

ARMOUR

By 1250 BC a Bronze-Age warrior would have carried a bronze sword, **mace** and spear. He would have been armed with a bronze helmet, chest and back plates and leg protectors (below).

MINING

By about 1200 BC everyday objects in Europe were made of bronze. Bronze is a mixture of copper and tin. Here you can see a cross-section of a copper mine. A shaft was dug to reach the copper which was then taken out with picks made from deers' antlers.

THE WORLD

THEIR LEGACIES

As the controlling chieftains of Bronze-Age Europe became richer a new class of people emerged — the warrior class. We do not know the names of individuals or peoples because this was still a period of prehistory. But we do know that different tribes, or nations, can be identified from the remains of their settlements and burials. During this period boundaries began to be set between peoples and their lands.

WASSERBURG

In what is now called the Federsee Lake in Germany is an island called Wasserburg (below right). Around 1200 BC it was a small village of about 40 wooden houses. The villagers kept cattle, sheep, pigs, goats and horses. They hunted wild boar, **elk**, bear and deer and fished for pike and catfish.

FOSSUM

In southern Scandinavia there were farming settlements similar to those in other parts of Europe at that time. This rock engraving (above) from Fossum in Sweden shows two warriors on a ship.

CARNAC

The most impressive stone monuments in Europe can be found at Carnac in north-western France (above). Each group of stones is made up of between 10 and 13 parallel rows stretching for several kilometres and consisting of nearly 3,000 upright stones.

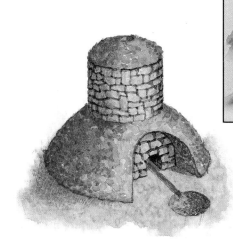

SMELTING

The metal needed to make tools and weapons comes from ores — parts of rocks which contain metal. To extract the metal, the ore is heated in a furnace (above). This is called smelting.

During the Bronze Age fragments of ore were laid over wood and then a fire was lit. The melted copper then ran out in the groove you can see here as molten (liquid) metal. It was then reheated with tin and poured into stone moulds.

A bronze incence burner stand from Cyprus

TRADE

We know that there was a lot of contact between the peoples of Bronze-Age Europe. Tools, weapons and armour of the same type has been found in many different countries. Archaeologists have also discovered objects made of materials which can only be found in far-off countries. For example, **amber**, which comes from around the Baltic Sea has been found in Mycenae (see pages 36–7). An enormous amount of copper was mined in Austria and exported all over Europe. Tin from Cornwall, France, Spain and northern Italy were also traded widely.

STONEHENGE

BC
- c. 3000 First phase of the circular ditch with four stones inside
- c. 2100 80 bluestones brought to make a double circle, never completed
- c. 2000 Huge sarsen stones brought to make the outer circle and a central horseshoe shape

- c. 1550 Bluestones rearranged into horseshoe shape in the centre and a circle. Two circles of holes dug outside the sarsen ring
- c. 1100 The avenue which approaches Stonehenge was extended

There are over 900 stone circles in Britain alone and Stonehenge (right) is probably the most famous stone circle in the world. The farming community which built it in about 3000 BC must have been very rich in order to spare so many people for its construction. The community must also have been well organized. Like most other stone circles the site itself was very carefully measured out. We think that Stonehenge was built as some sort of temple for ceremonies and religious rituals. Some experts believe that Stonehenge was built to make observations of the planets and stars. Careful placing of the stones, perhaps after a year of observation, would have given farmers a sort of calendar. Calculations would tell them when the seasons, and the ceremonies which went with them, were due to be held.

CONSTRUCTION TOOLS

This pickaxe is made from a deer's antler and this shovel was an ox's shoulder blade. The hammer stones pounded the stones into shape.

HOW STONEHENGE WAS BUILT

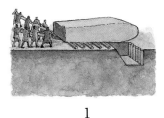

1

The huge stones were moved on wooden rollers to holes which had already been dug with bone and antler tools.

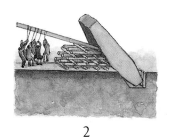

2

The far side of the hole was protected by timbers to stop it breaking down as the stone was levered into place.

3

The stone could then be hoisted up and pushed upright with wooden poles into its foundation hole.

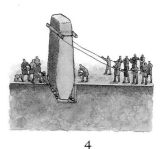

4

The hole was filled in with used hammer stones and chalk which was packed down hard.

BC
c. 3000 First evidence of
hieroglyphic writing
Dingo (dog) introduced into
Australia
c. 2500 City-states in Sumeria
First large settlements in the
Andes region
c. 1900 Indus Valley Civilization in
decline

THEIR ACHIEVEMENTS
Archaeologists working on stone circles have discovered that most of them were very carefully measured. Their builders obviously knew how to measure. But did they use standard measurements, as we do today? Some experts believe they did and one engineer, Professor Alexander Thom, suggested that they were built with a standard measurement of 0.829 metres. However, this measurement does not apply to all the circles in Britain, Ireland and other parts of Europe.

c. 1700 New palaces built on Crete
1339 Pharaoh Tutankhamun
buried
c. 1200 First civilizations in
Mesoamerica
c. 1000 Phoenician alphabet
introduced
Kingdom of Israel ruled by
King David

Stonehenge is not a single circle of stones. The larger stones which form the great arches are called sarsen stones (the largest weighs about 50 tonnes). They were brought from the downs of Wiltshire which are 30 kilometres away from Stonehenge. The smaller stones, called bluestones, weigh about 4 tonnes each and were transported overland and by sea from the Preseli Mountains of South Wales, which are over 200 kilometres away.

5
The outer ring of stones was made from two upright stones with a stone laid across the top (called a lintel).

6
The heavy lintel was slowly rolled into position and gradually raised on top of huge timbers.

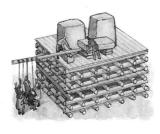

7
Levers were used to raise the stone at each end so that other timbers could be put underneath it.

8
Finally, the lintel reached the top and could be levered into position across the two upright stones.

THE SCYTHIANS

The Scythians were a nomadic people who probably originally came from Central Asia (modern-day Armenia, Russia and the Balkans) in the eighth century BC. They migrated south and occupied the land around the Black Sea and the Caspian Sea. Whole groups travelled with their possessions in felt-covered waggons in search of land to graze their cattle, sheep and horses. In the western part of Scythian territory there were some heavily-fortified permanent settlements. The Scythians were a warlike people whose warriors rode horses (like the one below) into battle. We know about the Scythians because of their contact with the Greeks. The Greek historian, Herodotus, wrote that they were fierce warriors whose women... '...take part in war and wear the same clothes as men. They have a marriage law which forbids a girl to marry until she has killed an enemy in battle'.

This is a drawing of a horse that was sacrificed and buried with its owner. The horse is wearing a ceremonial harness, tailpiece and saddle.

BURIAL TOMBS

Most of the information we have about what the Scythians looked like and the things they used comes from burial chambers which have been excavated. Tombs, like the one below from Pazyryk in the Altai Mountains of Siberia, were rooms constructed with large painted timbers. This fifth century BC burial chamber contained a fine waggon which had been dismantled. Other tombs contained slaughtered horses and servants. Above the burial chamber a great mound was built from soil and grass cut from high-quality **pasture** land.

BC
c. 750 Greek colonies in the Mediterranean
c. 500 Cast iron first used in China for farm tools and weapons
c. 400 Olmec civilization in decline
327–325 Alexander the Great campaigns in India
146 Greece made into Roman provinces
c. 100 North Vietnam ruled as a Chinese province

THEIR ACHIEVEMENTS

*Herodotus described the Scythians as, 'people who take their dwellings with them and are without exception the best archers on horseback. They do not farm but breed animals. Their homes are their waggons.' The Scythians survived until the third century AD when they were wiped out by invading **Ostrogoths**.*

AD
c. 100 Kingdom of Axum in Ethiopia established
Paper first used in China
c. 150 Rise of the city of Teotihuacán in the Valley of Mexico

TRADE

The Greek Empire lay on the western edge of Scythian territory. Later, these same lands were conquered by the Romans. We know that the Greeks and Scythians traded with each other. Scythian nobles became very rich by selling huge quantities of corn to the Greeks. In return they bought luxury goods, such as drinking cups and bowls, dishes, buckets and *amphorae* (storage jars) full of wine. The Scythians also traded with the Far East. Chinese silk has been found in some Scythian tombs — perhaps the Scythians acted as **agents** for goods brought from the Far East before they were passed on to the peoples of the Mediterranean and western Europe.

ART

The Scythians were fond of brightly-coloured clothes and beautiful objects. This comb (above) is made of gold and shows the Scythians in battle. The warrior on horseback has wounded his opponent's horse (on the right) and another man on the left is entering the fight. This comb was found in the tomb of a rich man and would probably have been a decorative comb used to hold his long hair together.

There was decoration everywhere in Scythian society. Their tents were lined with hangings and there were decorative cushions and carpets on the floor. One carpet, measuring 1.8 metres by 2 metres, was made by the hand-knotting technique — one and a quarter of a million knots were tied to make complicated patterns and pictures of horses, warriors and elks. The bronze cauldrons they cooked in were often decorated with battle scenes or with pictures of animals.

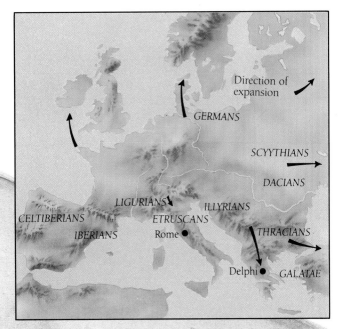

This is a Scythian wine jug. It shows Scythian warriors taming wild horses for use in battle.

TATTOOING

The Scythian tombs at Pazyryk in the Altai Mountains have been very well preserved because they have been protected by a layer of ice since about 400 BC. Even the skins of the human bodies were preserved and showed that some people were tattooed. Herodotus wrote that, *'the Scythians consider that tattooing is a mark of noble birth'*. The man drawn above was found in a burial at Pazyryk. He probably died in battle — his body has three battle-axe wounds. The enemy had already cut off his head — the Scythians scalped their enemies and used part of the skull as a drinking bowl. Most of his body had been tattooed with pictures of animals and fish.

THE CELTS

The Celts lived in western Europe from about 700 BC. We know quite a lot about them from their remains and from the ancient Greeks and Romans who wrote about them. Various ancient writers tell us that they were an excitable people. The Greek writer Strabo said that Celtic warriors were *'mad keen on war, full of spirit and quick to begin a fight'*. Another historian, called Diodorus Siculus, described Celtic fashion, *'They wear striking clothing, tunics dyed and embroidered in many colours and trousers called* bracae. *They wear striped cloaks, fastened with a brooch, thick in winter and light in summer, in a* **variegated**, *close-set check pattern.'*

The Celts moved across Europe in search of new lands to conquer. They invaded Italy in the fifth century BC and even raided Rome, the capital of the Roman Empire, in 390 BC. But they were not just gangs of invading warriors. In the west of Europe they lived in defended hilltop settlements, in villages and on isolated farms. They farmed the land, grew a great variety of crops and kept animals.

The back of a Celtic mirror

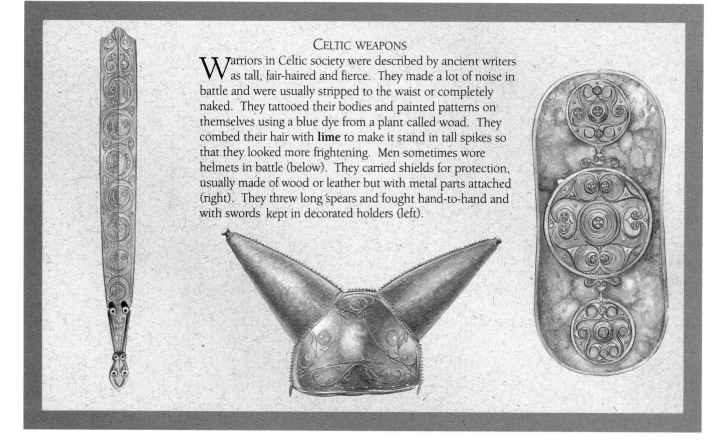

CELTIC WEAPONS

Warriors in Celtic society were described by ancient writers as tall, fair-haired and fierce. They made a lot of noise in battle and were usually stripped to the waist or completely naked. They tattooed their bodies and painted patterns on themselves using a blue dye from a plant called woad. They combed their hair with **lime** to make it stand in tall spikes so that they looked more frightening. Men sometimes wore helmets in battle (below). They carried shields for protection, usually made of wood or leather but with metal parts attached (right). They threw long spears and fought hand-to-hand and with swords kept in decorated holders (left).

BC
814	Phoenicians found the new city of Carthage in north Africa
627	Assyrian Empire at its largest size
c. 500	First Chinese coins

THEIR LEGACIES

Even after the Romans conquered western Europe in the first century BC and drove the Celtic peoples further west, Celtic traditions survived. Traces of Celtic tradition can be found today in several languages which survived the Roman occupation — Breton in Brittany in northern France, Cornish in Cornwall, Welsh in Wales and Gaelic in parts of Scotland and Ireland.

333	Alexander the Great defeats the Persians at the Battle of Issus
214	Great Wall of China begun
146	Carthage destroyed by the Romans
100	Okvik hunting peoples settle in Alaska

MAIDEN CASTLE

This Celtic town (above) was defended by huge banks, ditches, wooden fences and strong gates.

HEUNEBURG

Heuneburg (above) in modern day Germany was the home and court of a noble Celtic prince who imported fine Greek and Etruscan objects.

Artists carved human heads which give us a good idea of what people looked like (below). Their long, flowing moustaches, said one ancient writer, *'become mixed with food and act as a sort of strainer for the drink to pass through'.*

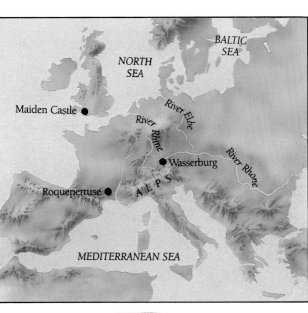

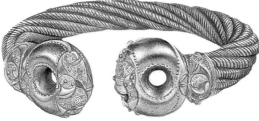

CELTIC ART

We know that Celtic clothes were bright and colourful but skilled craftspeople also made a number of highly-decorated objects. Favourite or important possessions, such as mirrors and weapons, must have taken great skill to make. Most decorated Celtic objects were made of metals such as bronze, iron, gold and silver. Really precious objects, such as torcs (neckbands) were made of solid gold (above). Many other objects were decorated in Celtic times apart from weapons — brooches, hairpins, rings, horse harness fittings and horse armour, for example. Metal was decorated in different ways — either incised (scratched) on the surface or hammered in. Some metal objects were coloured with paints for extra decoration. Although many objects were just decorated with patterns, Celtic people also liked objects with animal designs on them. Horses were often used to decorate coins but other animals such as cats, wild boar, dogs, birds, rams and cows also appear.

HELVETII

This Celtic tribe tried to move from their own territory but were forced back by the Romans in 58 BC.

RELIGION

The Celts cut off their enemies' heads and placed them in a column at the front of a shrine at Roquepertuse (above).

Celtic art survived long after Britain was freed from the Romans. This is a decorated page from the *Book of Kells* (below) made in Christian Ireland in the early ninth century AD. Compare this decoration with other Celtic objects on these pages.

CITY PLANNING
Farming people began to settle in the Indus Valley around 3500 BC. Mohenjo-daro was the largest city of the Indus Valley Civilization. The city was carefully built to a plan and houses were connected to the city's sewage and waste disposal systems.
See pages 64–5.

SEAL STONES
We know that there was a great deal of contact between the cities of the Indus Valley and other places, such as the Persian Gulf, because of trade. Merchants used carved stones to put a seal on bales (bundles) of goods such as cotton and spices.
See page 65.

A STONE CITY
Great Zimbabwe is the largest ancient building of Black Africa. The city reached the height of its power around AD 1350. Huge stone structures were built there, including some walls ten metres high. Zimbabwe (the name of the modern country) comes from the **Shona** language dzimba dza mabwe meaning 'houses of stone'.
See page 71.

JENNE-JENO
The remains of Africa's oldest city, Jenne-jeno, can be found in the modern state of Mali. Some of the houses of Jenne-jeno were built in a traditional round style but others were square or rectangular. African houses are usually circular so these rectangular houses show the influence of African trade with the peoples of the Near East.
See page 70.

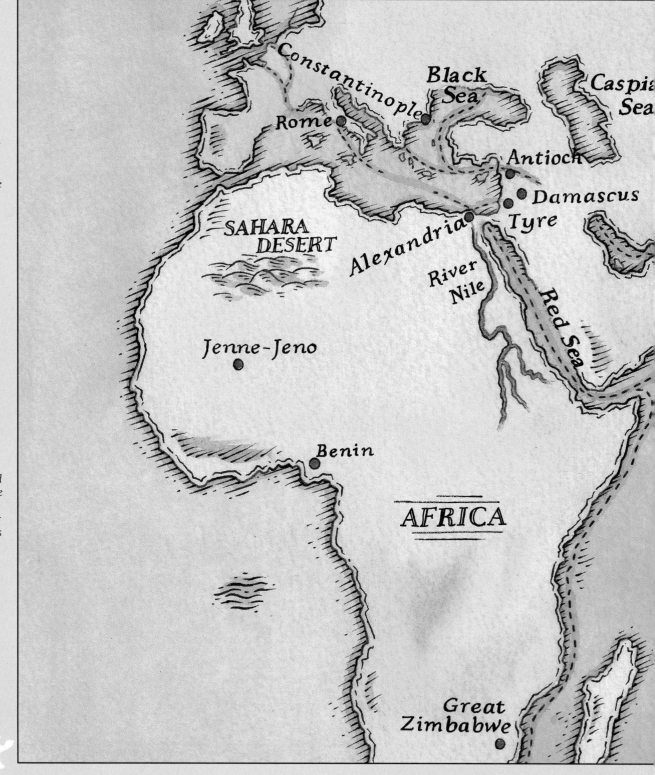

RICH KINGDOMS
The kingdoms of west Africa were very wealthy. They traded north across the Sahara Desert and south-west within the continent itself. Thousands of beautiful objects were made out of gold, brass and ivory.
See page 70.

MYSTERIOUS SILK
Silk was a prized cloth from Greek times onwards. People in the West could not understand how it was made. It was exported from China to as far away as Britain.

AFRICAN EXPORTS

Many of the peoples of Africa exported goods to Arabia, China and India. Arab sailors and merchants settled along the east coast of Africa and set up trading stations. The Arabs acted as middlemen — this means that they bought goods off African merchants and sold them on to foreign traders who visited the busy ports of the African coastline.

HOUSES WITHOUT WINDOWS

There were no windows in the outside walls of houses in Indus Valley towns — only the door opens on to the street. There were windows inside the house facing into a central courtyard. When it was very hot people slept outside on the flat roofs — just as people do today in hot countries. See page 64.

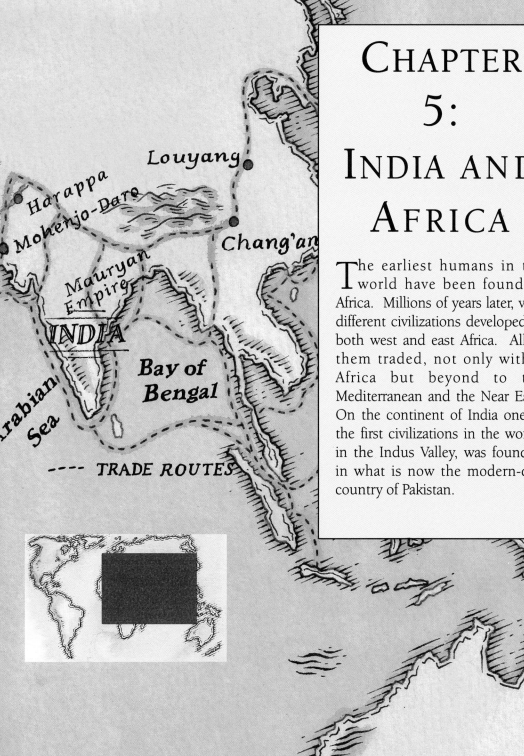

CHAPTER 5:

INDIA AND AFRICA

The earliest humans in the world have been found in Africa. Millions of years later, very different civilizations developed in both west and east Africa. All of them traded, not only within Africa but beyond to the Mediterranean and the Near East. On the continent of India one of the first civilizations in the world, in the Indus Valley, was founded in what is now the modern-day country of Pakistan.

EMPERORS AND VICEROYS

The emperors of the Mauryan Empire governed their lands through viceroys who each toured their own province to make sure that everything was in order. The emperor even sent his own inspectors to make sure his viceroys were doing their jobs. The people, who were mostly farmers, paid taxes to the emperor.
See page 66.

BUDDHISM

It was during the time of the Mauryan Empire of India that the religion of Buddhism was really established, although the Buddha himself, Siddhartha Gautama, had been born around 566 BC. The first Buddhist monuments and monasteries were built during the reign of Emperor Asoka. See page 67.

SELLING SILKS AND SPICES

A series of caravan routes stretched from China to the Mediterranean carrying silk and many other luxury goods such as pottery, metalwork, ivory and spices. Goods were also carried to the West by sea, around India and to Europe via the Red Sea and the Persian Gulf. See pages 68–9.

BUDDHIST MONKS

Buddhist monks lived in communities in monasteries. The most important part of each monastery was the stupa. It was here that the sacred objects of the religion were kept and rituals held. The stupa was originally a simple earth mound. Over time it changed into a mound-shaped stone building.
See page 67.

THE INDUS VALLEY CIVILIZATION
BC
c. 3500 First farming villages in the
Indus Valley
c. 2500 Indus Valley Civilization
established
Cities of Mohenjo-daro and
Harappa built

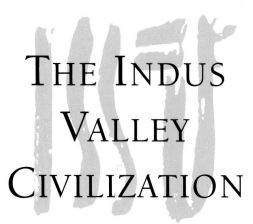

THE INDUS VALLEY CIVILIZATION

c. 1900 Civilization begins to
decline, houses neglected,
irrigation systems fall into
disrepair
c. 1700 Civilization collapses
c. 1500 Aryans arrive in northern
India

The Indus Valley Civilization of ancient India is named after the River Indus, in the modern-day country of Pakistan. A number of large cities were built along the Indus River around 2500 BC. An archaeologist, called R. D. Banerjii, discovered the city of Mohenjo-daro (below) in 1922. The cities of this earliest Indian civilization were carefully planned and contained hundreds of houses, shops, public buildings and workshops. The cities were defended by surrounding brick walls. The first farmers settled in this area around 3500 BC. It was an area full of wildlife and the land was rich and suitable for growing crops because the rainfall was higher than it is now. The people of the Indus Valley grew wheat, barley, vegetables and, in some places, rice. They kept animals such as cattle, sheep, pigs, dogs and buffaloes. They probably used horses, elephants and camels for farming, trade and travel. Around 1900 BC the climate altered and over the next few hundred years floods destroyed good farming land and mud clogged up the coastline. Places which had once been busy harbour cities found themselves inland. The cities fell into disrepair and people moved to small farms.

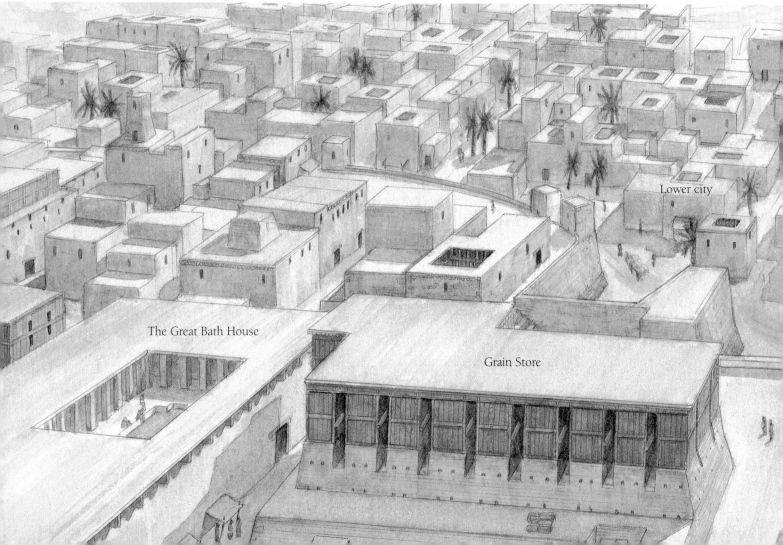

The Great Bath House

Lower city

Grain Store

BC
- c. 3500 Llama first used as a pack animal in Peru
  First city civilizations established in Sumeria
- c. 3000 Coastal regions of Australasia occupied by hunters and fishers
  First evidence of Egyptian hieroglyphic writing

THEIR ACHIEVEMENTS

The people of the Indus Valley built the world's first sewage system. Under the regularly laid-out streets, brick drains carried waste from houses and workshops out of town. The drains could be checked at regular intervals through inspection chambers at street level. The streets were also probably guarded by police — little buildings like sentry boxes have been found at street corners.

- c. 2300 Settlements in Mesoamerica
- c. 2000 First settlers in New Guinea
  Inuits (Eskimos) reach northern part of Greenland
- c. 1450 Eruption on island of Thera
  End of Minoan civilization

MOHENJO-DARO

This city covered an area of about 60 hectares and had a population of about 40,000 people. The buildings were constructed from mud-bricks baked in the sun — the bricks were exactly the same size in all of the Indus Valley cities.

HARAPPA

Further to the north-east on one of the **tributaries** of the River Indus was the other main Indus Valley city, Harappa. This city was similar to Mohenjo-daro but smaller with a population of about 25,000 people.

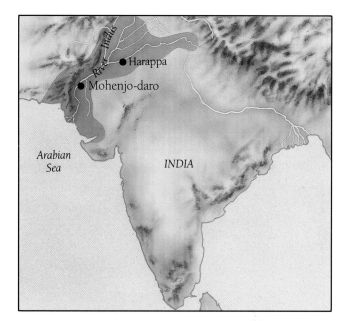

Arabian Sea

INDIA

CITIES

On the left is a drawing of the city of Mohenjo-daro. In the centre of the city there was a huge raised mound with public buildings on it — a great bath-house which was probably used in religious rituals, a wooden grain store 45 metres long, an assembly hall and a temple. The people of Mohenjo-daro lived in the lower town. Most people lived in one-room apartments. The rich lived in large two-storeyed houses (above). Rooms were grouped around an open courtyard. Some houses had their own water supply and lavatories. Houses were connected to a sewage system and had rubbish disposal points on their outside walls.

TRADE

The cities were major centres of trade. Each city had a huge number of workshops making pottery and metal tools, jewellery and cloth. We know there was trade between the Indus Valley, the Persian Gulf and Mesopotamia. There were also overland trade routes to Persia and Afghanistan. There was a standard system of weights and measures. Bales of goods for shipment were marked with seals like the one below. The writing is hieroglyphic but it has not been deciphered — perhaps it records the name of the merchant or company shipping the goods.

This **bust** of a bearded man (below) was found in Mohenjo-daro. He was probably a priest or a king.

THE MAURYAN EMPIRE

Sometime around 1500 BC people, called Aryans, arrived in north-west India. They dominated the people who were there before them and built large cities. Gradually they spread east and settled on the land of the upper Ganges. By 600 BC there were at least 16 small states in the plain of the River Ganges. In the next century these states were constantly at war with each other. The strongest state took control of the others and eventually they were all taken over by the Kingdom of Magadha. At the end of the fourth century BC the kingdom was seized by Chandragupta Maurya. He was the first real emperor of India and his territory, the Mauryan Empire (left), stretched over most of the continent of India.

Chandragupta's grandson, Emperor Asoka, came to power in 269 BC and made the empire even bigger. He kept very close control of his lands. The people, most of whom were farmers, paid taxes to him. These taxes paid for things like the road system, the civil servants who organized the state and Asoka's huge conquering army.

Map labels: HINDU KUSH, GANDHARA, Kandahar, Taxila, HIMALAYAS, River Indus, NEPAL, THAR DESERT, River Ganges, Pataliputra, Sanchi, MAGADHA, DECCAN, Arabian Sea, Gulf of Cambay, KALINGA, Maski, Bay of Bengal, Mysore, Indian Ocean, SRI LANKA

TRADE

There was trade throughout the different states of the Mauryan Empire and with other countries. The Romans imported many goods from India at this time, including ivory, cotton cloth, spices (below) and precious stones. Roman writers tell us about trade with India and there were even Roman trading stations on the southern coasts of the continent. The Roman writer **Pliny** wrote that it was '*40 days voyage from the Red Sea to the first trading station in India, which was called Muziris*'.

FARMING

The people of the Mauryan Empire were farmers but the land they farmed was actually owned by the emperor. People paid taxes on the land they farmed, the crops they produced and the animals they reared. The emperor could order land to be cleared for agriculture and moved people by force from one place to another if the population became too large. Irrigation was essential if the land was to be farmed properly . Rivers were **dammed** and **reservoirs** created. Canals took water to irrigate terraces like these on the right. When irrigation schemes were provided by the state, the farmers had to pay an extra water tax.

BC
c. 1500 Mycenaean civilization established
c. 1000 Phoenician alphabet introduced
Kingdom of Israel ruled by King David
c. 900 Chavín civilization in the Andes, south America

THEIR LEGACIES
*The Mauryan Empire was responsible for two very important events. One affected the boundaries of the **subcontinent** of India — for the first time in this part of the world huge numbers of people were controlled and governed as one country. After Emperor Asoka's death his great empire began to break up. The other significant event of this period — Buddhism — is still with us today. The Buddhist religion spread to many eastern countries. Today there are over 500 million followers of Buddhism.*

509 Last Etruscan king, Tarquin the Proud, expelled by the Romans
c. 400 Celts migrate into northern Italy
334 Alexander the Great begins his campaigns against the Persians
250 All of Italy is controlled by the Romans

BUDDHISM

One of the world's greatest religions, Buddhism, was founded in India during the time of the Mauryan Empire. Siddhartha Gautama was born around 566 BC into a rich family. At the age of 29 he saw four signs which changed his life. He decided to leave home and search for what he called the True Wisdom. After six years he reached *Nirvana*, or **enlightenment**, and became the 'Buddha' which can be translated as the 'Enlightened One'. For the next 45 years he preached a very simple philosophy — that Nirvana could be reached by doing good works and **meditating**. After his death a group of followers established an order of Buddhist monks to spread Siddhartha's beliefs. Buddhism spread beyond the Mauryan Empire to South East Asia, China and Japan.

A statue of Buddha in India (top) and modern-day Buddhist monks in India (above).

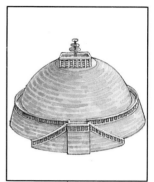

The Great Stupa at Sanchi, in India.

The stupa at Borobodur, in Java.

Stupa at Sarnath in India

MONASTERIES AND STUPAS

The Emperor Asoka converted to Buddhism and it became the main religion of his empire. The emperor helped spread the religion by ordering Buddhist inscriptions to be carved on to flat rock surfaces and specially-made pillars. He also helped build monasteries for Buddhist monks. In the centre of each monastery was a special building called a stupa (left and below) for the rituals of the religion. The first stupas were simple mounds of earth but later were made into round stone buildings. Temples were built to cover the small stupas which often contained holy relics. As Buddhism spread stupa buildings became more elaborate and were often decorated with statues and carvings.

THE SILK ROAD

BC

c. 550 First silks appear in the West, in Greece

c. 100 Silk Road fully open from China to the West

AD

c. 250 Sassanians control much of the trade in spices

618– Tang Dynasty in China
907 Silk Road traffic increases

651 Muslims control the silk and spice routes

1405 Silk Road trade in decline China explores sea routes for spice trade

1450 Chinese Ming rulers cut links with the outside world

1514 Portuguese ships arrive in China for the first time

The most important trade route in Asia and Europe was called the Silk Road. It stretched from China to the waters of the Mediterranean. We know that Chinese silk had reached Greece by 550 BC. But it was not just silk that was traded along this route. Many other luxury goods were carried as well, including fine pottery and spices. The Silk Road was not actually a road at all but a series of caravan routes between towns and desert **oases**. Goods were also transported by sea from the Far East, around India and through the Persian Gulf or the Red Sea.

ITALY
Rome

GREECE

Mediterranean Sea

Black Sea

Ephesus

TURKEY

Caspian Sea

Tyre

IRAQ

IRAN

Arabian Sea

INDIA

GLASSWARE

The **Sogdian** people, who lived in the Samarkand region of central Asia, were merchants in the middle of the Silk Road. They traded goods brought from the Far East but also made their own objects and materials. They made the glass vessels drawn above in the eighth century AD.

BC	
508	Democratic government established in Athens
c. 200	Nazca civilization at its height
30	Egypt made a Roman province

AD	
29	Jesus Christ crucified
100	Paper first used in China
330	New capital of Roman Empire founded at Constantinople

THEIR LEGACIES

The Silk Road helped far-off lands to communicate. Ideas as well as goods were carried from the Far East and from the West. People in the Roman Empire wanted to buy exotic eastern goods. Cooking in western Europe was influenced and changed by the introduction of new Far-eastern spices. Several peoples still trade in the goods their ancestors sold along the Silk Road hundreds of years ago.

450	Teotihuacán becomes the sixth-largest city in the world
1096	First western Christian Crusade to the Holy Land
1347	Black Death begins to sweep through Europe
c. 1350	Maori people in New Zealand build fortified settlements
1492	Christopher Columbus reaches the Bahamas

CERAMICS

Today we use the word china for fine pottery objects, such as plates and cups. This plate (above) was copied from ancient Chinese designs. It was made in Worcester in England in the nineteenth century.

METALWORK

This drinking cup (above) was made during the **Tang Dynasty** (in about AD 730). Its decoration shows that the Chinese artist was influenced by designs introduced from the **Sassanian Empire** of Africa.

SILK

The Chinese discovered how to make the finest cloth in the world from silkworms. The two pieces above were made in China around the eighth century AD. At first only Chinese silk reached the West. Then other people, like the Sogdians, wove silk cloth from Chinese threads. In the sixth century AD, the Persians brought silkworms from China to the Byzantine court.

Xi'an

HIMALAYA

CHINA

Pacific Ocean

SPICES

Exotic flavourings extracted from plants were carried to western Europe from as near as Arabia and as far away as the islands of the Pacific Ocean. Spices like nutmeg (above) were used in cooking, perfumes, cosmetics and medicine.

AFRICA

AD
- c. 100   Kingdom of Axum established
- c. 400   First towns built south of the Sahara Desert
- c. 450   Iron-working by the Nok people of west Africa
- c. 500   Arrival of Bantu people
- c. 700   Kingdom of Ghana
  Arabs begin trading with African cities south of the Sahara Desert
- c. 750   Jenne-jeno's city wall is completed

- c. 1000   West African trading towns flourish
- 1054   Muslim conquest of west Africa begins
- c. 1200   Kingdoms of Benin and Mali established
- 1324   King of Mali visits Cairo, Egypt
- c. 1350   Great Zimbabwe at its height
  Kingdom of Songhay established.
  A university is established at Timbuktu
- 1450   Great Zimbabwe in decline

The earliest ancestors of human beings came from Africa millions of years ago. There were wealthy and advanced civilizations in Africa centuries before any Europeans set foot on the continent. In the north, the Egyptian civilization influenced and traded with other peoples in the Mediterranean and within Africa. Further south, along the Red Sea, the Kingdom of Axum (see coin right) played an important part in trade with Rome and with the **Kushan Empire** in India. In west Africa a number of civilizations flourished and traded iron and gold north across the Sahara Desert and to the south-east. The kingdoms of east Africa built large cities and ports and traded with the Muslims, the Indians and the Chinese.

BENIN

Benin was an important kingdom in what is now southern Nigeria. It thrived in the eleventh and twelfth centuries and its capital city was called Benin. The king, who was also the religious leader, was called the *oba*. He lived with his courtiers in a great palace in the walled city of Benin. The people of Benin traded pepper, **palm oil**, ivory and slaves.

JENNE-JENO

From about AD 400 the people of Jenne-jeno were trading iron and gold north across the Sahara Desert and food with neighbouring peoples. There were around 1,000 houses inside its walls by about AD 1000.

IVORY

This highly-decorated ivory bracelet (above) is the work of a skilled **Edo** carver from Benin.

BRONZE

This bronze head (above) was cast by a **Yoruba** metalworker in the eighth century AD.

IGBO UKWU

On the left is a drawing of a burial of an important person found at Igbo Ukwu. He was probably a ruler or a priest of a small kingdom from the eighth to ninth centuries AD. He was buried sitting on a stool surrounded by expensive objects in a decorated wooden chamber. Five other people, thought to be slaves, were buried on top of his chamber — perhaps as sacrifices to accompany their master on his journey to the next life. The people of Igbo Ukwu exported ivory and food in exchange for copper from the Sahara Desert. They must also have traded with places much further away as beads imported from India have been found at this site.

THE WORLD

THEIR LEGACIES

*The vast continent of Africa produced very different cultures and civilizations — from Egypt, to Benin, to Great Zimbabwe. The kingdoms of east and west Africa traded throughout the rest of the known world. But some Arab and European countries began to exploit the peoples of Africa and took large numbers of them away as slaves. Nineteenth-century white **immigrants** who came across the ruins of Great Zimbabwe did not believe that they had been built by Black Africans.*

MEDITERRANEAN SEA

ATLANTIC OCEAN

Trade route

Fez

SAHARA DESERT

Timbuktu

Jenne-jeno

River Niger

River Nile

RED SEA

River Congo

River Zambezi

Great Zimbabwe

INDIAN OCEAN

Trade route

TRADE ROUTES

Arab traders used boats like these, called dhows, to carry goods from India to east Africa. Rulers in Islamic coastal cities, such as Kilwa, acted as trading agents for inland merchants.

CHINESE POTTERY

Pottery, like this Ming Dynasty bowl (above), was imported into Europe and Africa. This pottery was prized by the wealthy rulers of east African kingdoms.

GREAT ZIMBABWE

By AD 1200 people had begun building great stone structures at the city of Great Zimbabwe. The city reached its largest size by about AD 1350 when 10,000 people lived there and it was the capital of a large empire. Most of the people of Great Zimbabwe were cattle farmers but there were also skilled iron, copper and goldsmiths. We know that they traded with people from all over the world because Islamic and Chinese pottery (see right) has been found at Great Zimbabwe.

WOOD AND EARTH

Buildings of the Shang period were made by ramming dry earth between wooden shuttering. In the king's palace at the first Shang capital of Erlitou, timbers held up the overhanging thatched roofs and the strong entrance gateways.
See page 75.

PICTURES, WRITING AND ART

Like other ancient writing, the first Chinese writing was in the form of pictographs (called characters). This writing became very complex and thousands of characters were used — most of which are still in use today. The Chinese also invented calligraphy — beautiful writing considered to be an art form. Artists used brushes and ink to draw both pictures and words.
See page 74.

CLAY WARRIORS

The most incredible tomb excavated from ancient China is that of the First Emperor, Ch'in. Pits around his burial place contained thousands of full-size warriors made from pottery. Each one must have been modelled on a real person as they are all different. In earlier times in China real soldiers would have been sacrificed when the king died.
See pages 78–9.

JADE AND GOLD CLOTHES

*Rich and important people of the Han Dynasty were buried in a number of different ways. Underground tombs contained their preserved bodies and possessions. The bodies of Prince Liu Sheng and his wife, Tou Wan, were encased in suits made of thousands of pieces of **jade** carefully sewn together with gold wire.*

CHAPTER 6: CHINA

The first real civilization in China began around 1600 BC with the Shang Dynasty. For many years there was little contact between the people of China and the West. By the third century BC the many little kingdoms of China were unified into one large country and contact with the outside world was made through trade. The Chinese invented their own writing and measuring systems and laws. They built large cities and could grow enough food to support huge populations.

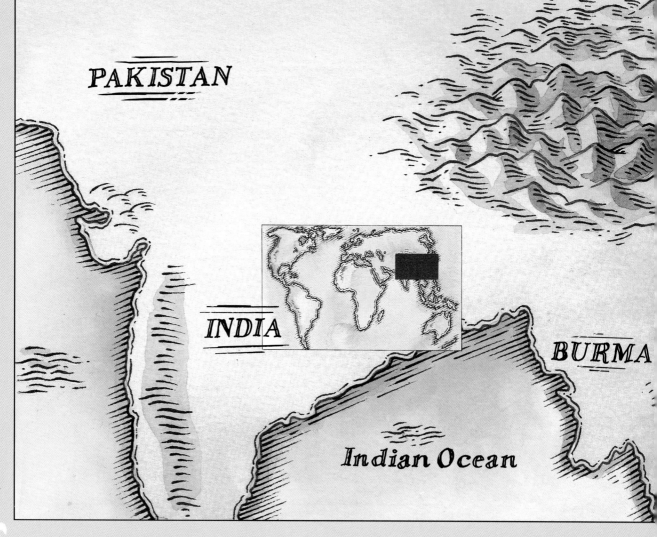

PAKISTAN

INDIA

BURMA

Indian Ocean

THE ART OF LACQUER

*Han artists were famous for the beautiful objects they made. One type of art, called lacquerwork, was made only in the Far East. Wooden objects such as bowls, cups and trays, were coated with a transparent (see-through) **lacquer**. The lacquer gives a shine to the object and brings out the colours. See page 78.*

THE SILK TRADE

During the Han Dynasty trade with the West became very important. The Silk Road (see pages 68–9) became a busy route. In the West, and especially in the Roman Empire, Chinese silk fetched high prices. In exchange, the Chinese wanted luxury goods such as furs, precious stones and ivory.

JADE AND METAL

Before metal was discovered, the Chinese used stone to make tools like axe heads. The stone had to be chipped into shape and then sanded smooth. Some axes were made from jade, which the Chinese liked to use for carving even after they had discovered bronze and iron.

BRONZE ANIMALS

Artists made very elaborate and beautiful objects from bronze during the Shang Dynasty. Bronze, a mixture of copper and tin, had to be heated in furnaces and poured into clay moulds. Animals were often featured on bronze objects and always had a significance.
See page 75.

ANYANG

Anyang was the final capital city of the Shang Dynasty. The capital had been in two other cities before. A wall ran right round the city to protect it and the houses and streets were laid out carefully inside. Outside the walls there were burial grounds and places for industries such as pottery making and metalworking.

MONGOLIA

THE GREAT WALL

JAPAN

●Anyang

CHINA

Yellow Sea

•••• SHANG CHINA
--- HAN EMPIRE

TAIWAN

Pacific Ocean

South China Sea

THAILAND

THE EMPEROR'S NAME

China got its name from Emperor Ch'in Shi-huang-ti. After centuries of fighting between small states and kingdoms, he emerged as the strongest leader. He ruthlessly forced other princes to obey him and united a vast area of land into one country. See pages 76–7.

A HUGE WALL

Perhaps the greatest building project ever undertaken was the Great Wall of China begun in 214 BC by Emperor Ch'in. He ordered a stone wall to be built across China's northern frontier to keep out the Barbarian tribes. Watchtowers provided extra security and were also used as signalling points to raise the alarm in time of war.
See page 76–7.

SHANG CITIES

At the height of its power the Shang Empire was made up of over 1,000 walled cities. All of these cities were connected in some way with the capital, Anyang.

THE SHANG DYNASTY

BC

1766 According to legend the first Shang king, T'ang, overthrows the Hsia Dynasty

c. 1600 Real beginning of the Shang Dynasty

c. 1400 Capital moves from Zhengzhou to Anyang

1400 12 kings rule from Anyang for 273 years

c. 1350 Oracle bone inscriptions

1027 Last Shang king, Chou Hsin, overthrown by the Chou people. Chou Dynasty begins

Civilizations in China developed on the fertile lands in the valleys of the Wei and Yellow rivers in northern China. Ruling families, called dynasties, controlled large areas of land. The people of the Shang Dynasty (1600–1027 BC) believed that their kings were descended from the supreme god, Shang Ti, who founded the world. The king was in control of everything and had a large army to back him up which was paid for from taxes collected from the people. Kings and queens were buried with large numbers of precious objects as well as sacrificed people and animals.

DAILY LIFE

Most people of the Shang Dynasty were farmers. The Shang kings were in charge of great irrigation schemes which allowed the fields to produce more crops. The main food crops were rice and **millet** but wheat was also grown. Farmers also kept animals such as cattle, sheep, horses, goats, pigs, chickens and dogs. Dogs were often sacrificed along with humans for the burials of Shang rulers. While most people lived in small farming settlements, there were also large towns and cities. Cowrie shells were imported from the Pacific and Indian oceans and were considered so precious that they were used as money.

This **ritual** vessel (left) was found in the tomb of a Shang king. It would have been filled with sweet-smelling wine as a gift to the king's ancestors.

WRITING

Chinese writing developed around 1500 BC. It was based on pictographs. But in China writing developed quite differently from the way it became used in other parts of the world. Each character showed both the sound of the word and its meaning. From around 1400 BC the Chinese engraved characters on oracle bones. These were animal bones or tortoiseshells on which questions were engraved. Questions were asked about important future events, a person's health or even the weather. The bones were heated in a fire and the cracks were interpreted as answers about the future. More and more characters were developed — by AD 100 there were about 9,000.

Characters were painted with a brush and ink on to paper, or engraved on bone or metal. These characters spell out the name Fu Hao. She was a member of the royal family and was buried at Anyang (see opposite).

THE WORLD

THEIR LEGACIES

The Shang Dynasty gave China its first real civilization. Many beautiful cities and palaces were built. Even in the twentieth century new Chinese buildings are being built which are based on the plan of a typical Shang palace. Bronze was first worked during this period and many of the shapes and designs first made by Shang metalworkers were copied by much later Chinese peoples.

ERLITOU

The earliest capital of the Shang Dynasty was at Erlitou. This is what the palace of the king is thought to have looked like (above). Like other royal palaces, it consists of wooden buildings on a raised earth platform.

A RICH WOMAN'S TOMB

This is the tomb of Fu Hao, the wife of a Shang king. Above her wooden coffin, hidden in its burial chamber, were the sacrificed bodies of 16 people and six dogs. One thousand-six hundred objects, mostly made of bronze, were also buried with her.

SHANG METALWORK

The Shang Dynasty is famous for its fine bronze metalwork. Good supplies of copper and tin could be mined near the capital cities. Most objects were made by pouring molten (liquid) bronze into moulds made of fired clay. Many objects were highly-decorated and very complicated to make. The Chinese believed that animals were able to communicate with their ancestors in the spirit world. Many objects, like this one on the left, have animals on them. The tiger is protecting the man and the vessel was used for pouring out liquids during religious or burial ceremonies. The vessel on the right is called a *ting* and was also used for preparing food during religious ceremonies.

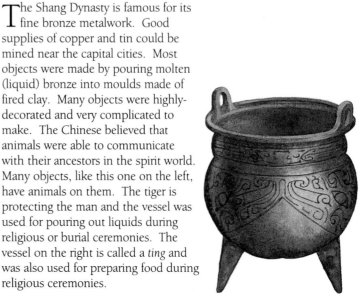

THE HAN DYNASTY

THE HAN DYNASTY

BC

246 Prince Cheng inherits a kingdom as a boy

221 Cheng crushes all resistance to his rule. He unites China and calls himself Ch'in Shi-huang-ti, 'the First Ch'in Emperor'

214 Great Wall of China begun

210 Ch'in dies

207 Ch'in Dynasty overcome by Liu Pang

207– Early Han Dynasty
AD 9

AD
9–23 Hsin Dynasty. Wang Mang takes control and becomes emperor

24– Eastern Han Dynasty
220

After centuries of **civil war** China was united under one emperor, Ch'in Shi-huang-ti, in 221 BC. China got its modern name from Emperor Ch'in. A census, or count, taken in AD 1 tells us that China had a population of 57 million people. This huge population was controlled from the capital city, called Chang'an. The emperor divided China into a number of provinces. Each province had its own governor and commander in charge of armed forces.

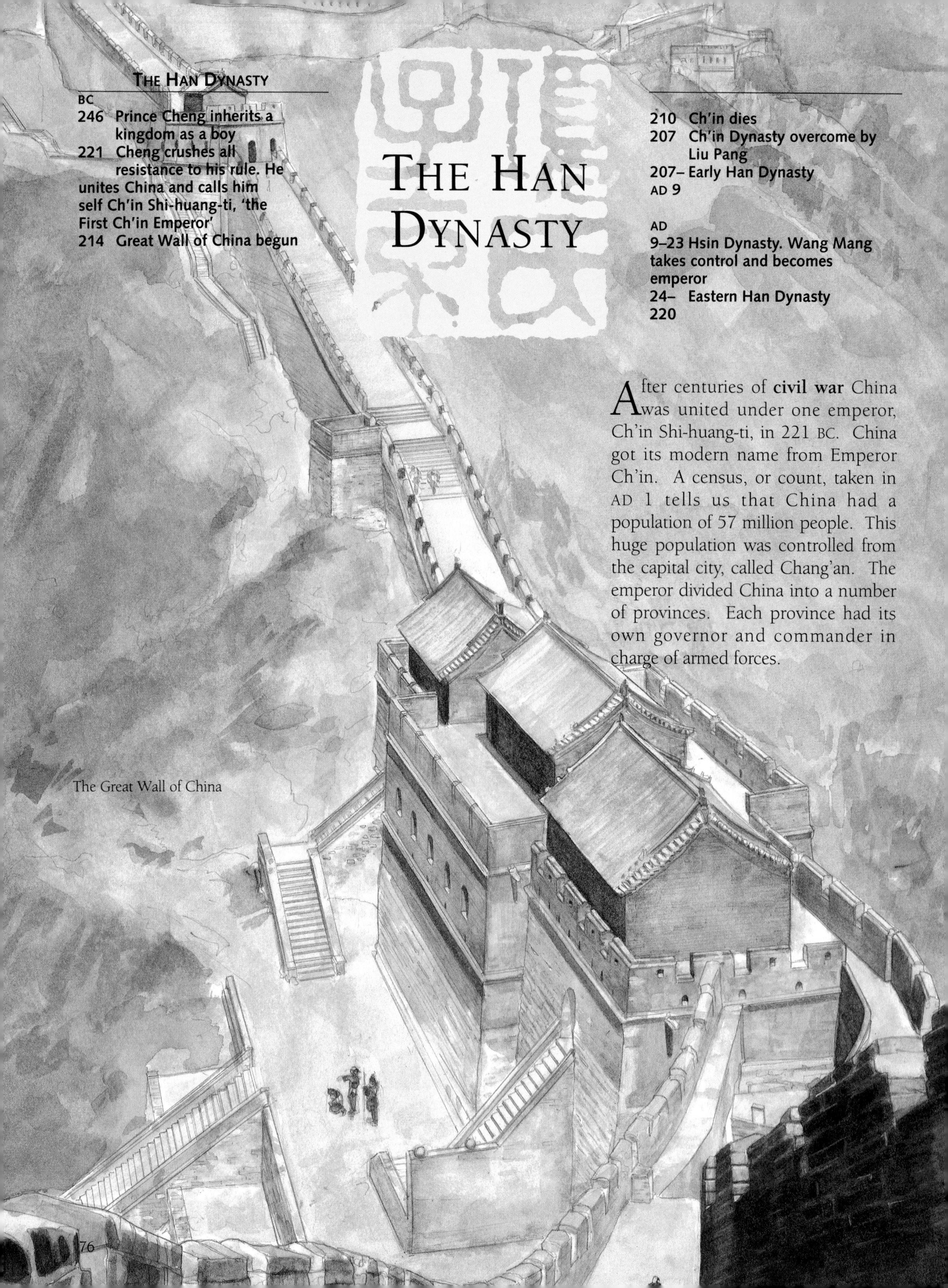

The Great Wall of China

BC

250	All of Italy is controlled by the Romans
c. 185	Mauryan Empire in India in decline
30	Egypt becomes a province of Rome

THEIR LEGACIES

The greatest achievement of Emperor Ch'in was to create one country — China — after years of war. He was not liked by the people or the nobles because he was very ruthless. Ch'in standardised many aspects of Chinese life — laws, writing, money, weights and measures — which continued in use long after his death. The First Emperor is probably best known today for building the Great Wall.

AD

29	Jesus Christ crucified
60	Kushan Empire established in India
79	Vesuvius erupts. Roman towns of Pompeii and Herculaneum destroyed
117	Roman Empire at its height
150	Rise of the city of Teotihuacán in the Valley of Mexico
224	Sassanid Dynasty established in Persia

EMPEROR CH'IN AND THE GREAT WALL

The full name of the Emperor Ch'in (above) meant 'the First Ch'in Emperor'. He established his own dynasty and died in 210 BC. But the system of government which Ch'in set up lasted in China until this century — in fact until 1912. Emperor Ch'in built a network of roads and canals across China and used his army to control any opposition to his rule. He also had to deal with threats of invasion from nomadic tribes to the north. Although there had been a series of earthen fortifications in northern China to keep out these 'Barbarians', Emperor Ch'in joined them together with a huge stone wall which became known as the Great Wall of China. It is the world's longest construction and stretches for about 2,300 kilometres. The wall is about 7.5 metres high and has watchtowers and defended gateways.

SILK WEAVING

One of the most important goods the Chinese traded was silk. Silk is a **fibre** from the cocoon of the silkworm. Each cocoon produces about 900 metres of fibre threads. When the threads have been cleaned, unwound and then twisted back together again, the very fine silk is woven on looms like this one into cloth.

HAN METALWORK

There were many skilled metalworkers in the Han Empire. Beautiful objects were often made from bronze. This horse is only 34.5 centimetres tall and is said to be 'flying' because it has one hoof on the back of a swallow. It was one of many fine objects excavated from a tomb.

EMPEROR CH'IN'S TOMB

BC

206	Han Dynasty founded by Liu Pang
c. 150	The Flying Horse sculpture is developed in the Kansu province of China

The painted wooden musician above was found in a Han Dynasty burial chamber.

AD

65	Envoys are sent to India to study Buddhism First Buddhist missionaries visit China
184	Uprising in China's Han Dynasty
190	The last Han emperor, Hsien-ti, takes the throne while still a boy
192	The boy-emperor is imprisoned
221	End of the Han Dynasty

Like many peoples in the world, the Chinese believed in life after death. They also believed that people would live the same sort of 'life' when they died. It was important, they thought, to take their possessions with them to the next life.

The tombs of the most important people in Chinese society were hidden deep under the ground and marked on the surface with great earth mounds. The tomb reconstructed below was 20 metres underground. We know from writings found with the body that it was the wife of the chief minister of the Kingdom of Changsha. To help preserve her body, it was wrapped in 20 layers of clothes and encased in four wooden coffins. Around the coffins were an enormous number of beautiful objects such as this lacquer tray (below), bowls, mugs and cups. There were fans, mirrors, clothes, boxes, little figures of her servants and food — chicken, sparrow, fish, rice and fruit.

The wooden coffins were preserved with a layer of solid white clay. The tomb was surrounded by a layer of charcoal.

THE TERRACOTTA ARMY
One of the most remarkable discoveries from the ancient world is the tomb of China's First Emperor, Ch'in. When Ch'in died he was buried under a huge mound of earth set inside a great courtyard. By the time of the First Emperor, servants were no longer sacrificed and buried with their masters and mistresses. Instead, thousands of life-size models of warriors were buried. You can see some of them in the photograph on the right. A Chinese historian tells us it took 700,000 forced labourers 36 years to build the tomb.

BC
c. 200　Alexandria develops as the centre of Greek science and learning

c. 100　Celts develop defended settlements
Farming settlements in the south-west of America

THEIR ACHIEVEMENTS

The tomb of the Emperor Ch'in was an incredible achievement. Each of the 7,000 pottery warriors, 3,000 footsoldiers, bowmen, spearmen and officers has a different face. There were also life-size pottery horses with their chariots. Some of the four burial pits of Emperor Ch'in's tomb were broken into long ago but in 1974 this pit (below), was discovered by accident, and found to be completely intact. It is being carefully excavated and preserved for people to see today.

AD
14　Roman emperor Augustus dies

c. 100　Kingdom of Axum established in Ethopia

c. 150　Rise of the city of Teotihuacán in the Valley of Mexico

224　Sassanid Dynasty established in Persia by Ardashir I

THE GIANT JAGUAR TEMPLE
Worship of the gods was very important for the Mayan people. They built huge stone temples in the form of pyramids. Look at page 82 to find the temple of the Giant Jaguar at Tikal in modern-day Guatemala.

WRITING WITH GLYPHS
Mayan writing was hieroglyphic. Inscriptions were carved outside temples and other public buildings. The longest Mayan inscription ever found has 2,500 glyphs and is in the city of Copán. Glyphs are often found on carvings and paintings giving the names of people. See page 82.

FRUITS AND DRUGS
European invaders put an end to the ancient civilizations of America with death and disease. In return they stole gold and silver objects which they melted down and shipped back to Europe. These invaders introduced some of our favourite fruits and vegetables, such as tomatoes and pineapples to Europe, as well as harmful drugs such as tobacco.
See page 87.

CHAPTER 7: THE AMERICAS

The first Americans hunted and gathered their food but by 7000 BC crops were being grown in Mexico. Advanced civilizations grew up in **Mesoamerica** — the Mayans, the Incas and the Aztecs. It was thousands of years before Europeans reached this continent. The first were the Vikings around AD 1000 who sailed to North America. From 1494 onwards the Spaniards and Portuguese arrived and divided the 'New World' between themselves.

THE END OF THE AZTECS
The moment the first Europeans arrived in the Americas its ancient civilizations were under threat. The Aztec emperor, Montezuma II, allowed the Spanish leader Hernán Cortés to enter his city because he believed Cortés to be the god, Quetzalcoatl. Cortés murdered Montezuma and destroyed the Aztec civilization.
See page 87.

MEXICO

Gulf of Mexico

Teotihuacán

Texcoco

Tenochtitlán

Mexico City

Metalwork from Mexican Highlands

Chichén Itzá

Uxmal

AZTECS

Monté Alban

MAYA

Palenque

Tikal

Metalwork from Central America

Santa Cruz

Copán

NICARAGUA

COSTA RICA

Pacific Ocean

AN EAGLE AND A SNAKE
*The capital city of the Aztec Empire was called Tenochtitlán, which means the 'Place of the Prickly Pear Cactus' in Quecha (the Aztec language). The name came from an incident in 1325 when the Aztecs were **migrating** to find a new home. An omen was seen — an eagle perched on the top of a cactus holding a snake — which told them where to found their city.*
See page 87.

HUMAN SACRIFICE
The Aztecs believed that the gods had sacrificed themselves as 'food' for the sun and the moon. They believed that human blood had to be offered to the gods to stop the world from coming to an end.
See page 86.

COUNTING AND SEEING INTO THE FUTURE
The Mayans had two complicated ways of measuring time. Their calendar began about 3114 BC by our system of measuring time. One calendar calculated days and months. The other calendar could only be understood by priests and was used to avoid doing things on days which were supposed to bring bad luck. See page 83.

BRILLIANT ASTRONOMERS
The Mayans built large cities. At Copán, in the modern-day country of Honduras priests watched the stars and the planets and were able to calculate the length of the month almost as accurately as astronomers do today.

Caribbean sea

Atlantic Ocean

PANAMA

VENEZUELA

COLOMBIA

PERU

BRAZIL

INCAS

● Machu Picchu

BOLIVIA

PARAGUAY

Pacific Ocean

Andes

URUGUAY

CHILE

ARGENTINA

Atlantic Ocean

INCA ROADS
The Incas built thousands of kilometres of roads across their empire to control their people and trade. Inca engineers were very clever at constructing bridges across deep gorges. There were no wheeled vehicles but the llama was used as a pack animal. See page 85.

BUILDING WITH STONE
*Machu Picchu is one of the most impressive sites of the ancient world. About 1,000 Inca people lived there, high in the mountains. Large blocks of hard granite were skilfully cut by masons to construct house and terrace walls. No mortar (cement) was used to hold the blocks in place and they were cut so that they fitted together perfectly.
See pages 84 and 85.*

AZTEC TEMPLES
Religion, and the rituals and ceremonies that went with it, were an important part of Aztec life. Large pyramid temples, called teocalli, were built inside sacred courtyards surrounded by a wall. There would also be other public and sacred buildings in the courtyard such as ball courts, racks to hold human skulls and temple schools. See page 86.

CUZCO, THE INCA CAPITAL
The Incas told the story that their capital city, Cuzco, had been founded by their first emperor, Manco Capac. Cuzco was the centre of the Inca Empire. The empire's 'four quarters', as they were called, radiated out from Cuzco's central plaza. Remains of many of Cuzco's buildings survive despite the destruction of the city by Spanish invaders in 1533. See pages 84–5.

THE MAYANS

BC
c. 2000 First Mayan peoples settle
c. 300– Mayan people influenced by Olmec
AD civilization
c. 300 Ceremonial centres built at places like Tikal
c. 300– Golden age of Mayan
c. 800 civilization Great cities built
615 Pacal becomes ruler of Palenque when 12

683 Pacal dies
c. 800 Lowland Mayan cities abandoned Civilization in decline
c. 980 Toltecs invade Mayan territory. Mayan civilization continues under Toltec rule
1200 Chichén Itzá abandoned
1328 Mayapan becomes the capital
1517– Spanish conquest of
41 Guatemala and Yucatán

For 600 years the Mayan civilization flourished in the part of the Americas we now call Mesoamerica or central America — the land which links north and south America. Mayan territory lies in the modern-day countries of Gautemala, Belize and Mexico. Mayan civilization reached its height around AD 300 when there were many large cities and religious centres with enormous public buildings. Mayan cities were all separate states with their own rulers. They were constantly at war with each other to capture their enemies to sacrifice to the gods.

The Giant Jaguar Temple at Tikal.

mol

xul

kayab

yaxkin

AGRICULTURE

Producing food was very important as there were as many as 50,000 people living in some Mayan cities. Mayan farmers grew a great variety of crops — **maize**, chilli peppers, squash and beans. To increase the amount of food they could grow, Mayan farmers developed a special irrigation system of small raised fields on the edges of swamps and rivers (left).

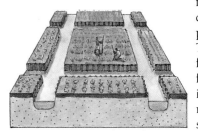

WRITING

The Mayas used a hieroglyphic system of writing (right). A series of 'glyphs' or pictures, gave the names of objects, rulers and cities. Glyphs were often carved or painted on stone. Four books, written on tree-bark paper have been found. We think that ancient Mayan writing may be similar to the language spoken by some Mayan people today.

tzec

muan

mac

kankin

BC
c. 2000 Minoan civilization on Crete
334 Alexander the Great invades Persian Empire
c. 100 Celts develop defended settlements
AD
79 Roman cities of Pompeii and Herculaneum destroyed by the volcano Vesuvius
c. 100 First use of paper in China

THEIR LEGACIES
The Mayans produced one of the most important civilizations in the Americas. They probably learned from an earlier civilization, the Olmecs, who lived just to the north of them. But unlike the Olmecs, the Mayans perfected writing and complex calendars. The earliest dated writing in the Americas comes from the early Mayan period. The Mayans are also famous for being the first peoples to construct huge stone-built cities.

300 Yamato state in Japan controls the whole country
475 Romulus Augustulus the last Roman Emperor in the West
c. 1000 Viking settlements in Labrador and Newfoundland
1202 Arab numerals introduced into Europe
1341 Black Death begins in Asia

MAYAN SCULPTURE
Mayan artists modelled stone, jade and clay. This figure (above) is from the burial island of Jaina, off the north coast of Mayan lands. Figures were made of gods, rulers and warriors.

RELIGION
Many religious beliefs were shared by the different peoples of the Americas. The Mayans worshipped a number of gods and built huge temples in their honour. They called the god who created their universe Itzam Na. There were gods of the sun and the moon, rain gods called *chaacs*, and individual gods for important aspects of Mayan life.

A sacred pyramid and statue in Chichén Itzá.

CHICHÉN ITZÁ
At the city of Chichén Itzá the Mayans built a round tower, 24 metres tall to watch the movements of the stars.

PALENQUE
In AD 615 a new ruler, called Pacal, took control of the city of Palenque . During Pacal's reign the city became the centre of a large state.

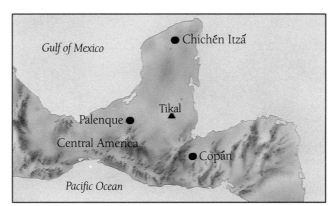

Gulf of Mexico
Chichén Itzá
Tikal
Palenque
Central America
Copán
Pacific Ocean

TIKAL
By the eighth century AD the city of Tikal had a population of around 50,000 people. There were five temple pyramids which were built on top of the tombs of past rulers of the city.

TWO CALENDARS
The Mayans had two calendars for calculating time. One was 365 days long and the other, a religious calendar, was made up of 260 days divided into 13 weeks of 20 days each. This sacred calendar was used to predict the future. The two wheels on the right show how the sacred calendar worked — the wheel on the left shows the 13 weeks, the one on the right the glyphs (or names) for each of the 20 days.

BALL COURTS
The centre of Mayan cities were large squares, or plazas, surrounded by huge buildings such as temple pyramids, palaces, great ceremonial causeways and ball courts. A ceremonial ballgame, called *tlachti*, was played all over Mesoamerica. The game was like modern basketball with two teams. But it was a rough game — players were often injured or killed.

THE INCAS

AD
- **c. 1200** Manco Capac founds the city of Cuzco
- **1438** Emperor Pachacuti extends the Inca Empire across Peru
- **1463– 71** Topa Inca, Pachacuti's son, conquers lands in central Chile

- **1476** The Chimú, in the north, are conquered. Their land becomes part of the Inca Empire
- **1493– 1525** Emperor Huayna Capac extends the empire to Colombia
- **1532** Inca Empire is destroyed by the Spanish led by Francisco Pizarro

The Incas grew from a small tribe, around AD 1200, into an enormous empire of eight million people along the Andes mountain range of South America (in modern-day Ecuador, Peru, Bolivia and Chile). According to Inca legend their first ruler, Manco Capac, founded the capital at Cuzco. The Inca leader was known as *Sapa Inca*, which means 'the only emperor'. In the fifteenth century AD Emperor Pachacuti extended Inca territory both north and south and by the next century the Inca Empire stretched from (modern-day) Ecuador to (modern-day) Chile. A large Inca army conquered new lands and kept people under control. Hostile peoples were forced to move into places in Inca territory where they could be supervised. The Incas called their empire *Tahuantinsuyu* which meant the 'Land of the Four Quarters'. The emperor appointed a governor to rule each quarter. Most Incas were farmers. They grew a wide range of food — from maize to beans, chilli peppers, potatoes, avocados and peanuts. People also ate pigs and ducks.

The Inca town of Machu Picchu.

THE INCA COUNTING SYSTEM

The Incas did not use writing but they did keep historical records. The *quipucamayoc* were state-appointed accountants who kept records on knotted cords, called *quipu*. These were cords of different colours with single, double or treble knots tied in them to mark events and accounts.

AD
- c. 1200 Rise of the Kingdom of Mali in west Africa
- 1241 Swedes now rule Finland
- 1309 Popular crusades launched in Europe
- c. 1350 Maori people on North Islands of New Zealand
- 1381 Peasants' Revolt in England

THEIR LEGACIES

Every person throughout the Inca Empire had to do some work for the state each year. It was known as mit'a and could involve labouring in the mines or on the roads or serving in the army. The invasion of the Spaniards (during the 1530s) put an end to the Inca Empire. But some parts of the ancient Inca civilization have survived. Most of the Indians who live in the Andes today still speak Quechua (the original Inca language) and those who look after herds still count them using the quipu.

- 1456 Ottoman Turks capture Athens
- 1497 Portuguese Vasco da Gama sails to India via the Cape of Good Hope
- 1516 Coffee is first imported into Europe

INCA ROADS

The Incas needed roads to control their empire. They were excellent engineers who built over 23,000 kilometres of roads. Government runners provided a 24-hour service carrying messages between relay stations (called *tambos*) about 2.5 kilometres apart.

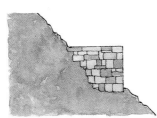

Roads (above) were built in straight lines where possible but they sometimes had to zig-zag up and down steep mountains.

Inca engineers had to continue roads across rivers and streams. They built suspension bridges made out of twisted plant fibres .

TRANSPORT

There were no wheeled vehicles anywhere in the Americas before the arrival of Europeans. Important officials, like the empire's governors, were carried on **litters**. In the Inca Empire goods were carried on peoples' backs or on animals such as llamas (above).

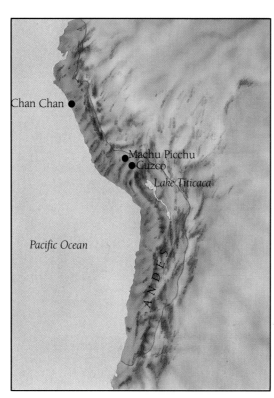

Chan Chan

Machu Picchu
Cuzco

Lake Titicaca

Pacific Ocean

ANDES

CUZCO

Modern-day Cuzco is built on top of the Inca capital planned by the Emperor Pachacuti in 1438 (right).

CHAN CHAN

The Chimú people lived on the desert coast of northern Peru. Chan Chan was their capital (above). They were eventually conquered by the Incas.

MACHU PICCHU

This fortress city was built on a rock ridge surrounded by mountains. The land on each side of the city was terraced into fields. About 1,000 people lived in one-roomed houses grouped around open courtyards. Granite stone was cut into irregular shapes for walls and buildings.

RELIGION

The Incas worshipped their own ancestors. Mummified bodies were taken out of their tombs to attend ceremonies. The most important of these ancestors were the emperors. The Incas believed that the emperor was a direct descendant of the sun god, called Inti. The Incas also worshipped Wiraqocha, the creator, Killa, the moon goddess, Illapa, the god of thunder, Pachamama, the earth goddess and Mamaqocha, god of the sea. Temples were built throughout the empire for the worship of the gods. The most important was in the capital city, Cuzco. The temple was called Qorikancha, the 'Temple of the Sun'. Ceremonies for the gods usually involved sacrifice of animals, such as llamas or guinea pigs, and offerings of food or cloth but, sometimes, humans were also sacrificed.

THE AZTECS

Aztec legend tells how they, the 'people of Aztlan' to the north-west, were ordered by their god, Huitzilopochtli, to migrate to new lands in about AD 1300. Eventually they settled on the shores of Lake Texcoco in the Valley of Mexico. Here they built their capital, Tenochtitlán (below). The Aztecs were very warlike. They fought endless battles with neighbouring peoples until they became the most powerful group in the area. By 1428 they controlled the whole of the Valley of Mexico. Around 1500 they were in charge of a huge empire of ten million people. The supreme ruler of the Aztecs was the emperor, called *Tlatoani*, meaning 'Speaker' in Quecha. The emperor was elected by the royal family, the priests and the most important warriors. The empire was very rich. Captured luxury goods, such as cloth, and other resources, such as gold, silver and precious stones, were carried by merchants into the cities of the empire. Around 60,000 people came to trade in Tenochtitlán every day.

RELIGION AND WAR

Most Aztec boys, but especially from the nobility, went to military schools from the age of ten. Some boys and girls went to religious schools but only the boys went on to become priests. Religion was an important part of everyones' lives. Hundreds of gods and goddesses were believed to be responsible for what happened to people, the land, the skies and the sea. Huge temples, like these at Tenochtitlán (below), were built to the gods. Human sacrifice was an essential part of these ceremonies. Wars were fought mainly to capture people to sacrifice to the gods.

WRITING

Most Aztec writing used pictograms — pictures which represented words (above). Pictograms were painted on paper made from the inner bark of the fig tree, or on animal skins or cotton cloth. This writing recorded taxes, religious ceremonies, histories, maps and plans.

AD
c. 1300	Rise of the kingdom of Benin in Nigeria
1350	Firearms first used in Europe
1368	Ming Dynasty founded in China
1381	Peasants' Revolt in England
1421	Capital of China moved to Beijing (Peking)
1453	Constantinople falls to the Ottoman Turks
1492	Columbus sails to the Bahamas from Europe

THEIR LEGACIES

When the Spanish invaders reached Mexico in 1519 they found a very advanced civilization. Although the Europeans were horrified at the human sacrifices in Aztec temples, they came to cities which were much larger than anything in Spain at the time. The Spaniards destroyed the Aztec Empire and imposed Christianity, a European way of life and the Spanish language on the country.

1492	Granada, the last Muslim stronghold in Spain, is reconquered by the Christians
1497	Portuguese Vasco do Gama sails to India around Africa
1520	Reign of Suleiman the Magnificent, the golden age of the Muslim Ottoman Empire
	Chocolate is first imported into Europe

THE VALLEY OF MEXICO

Aztec people were divided into two classes — the *pipiltin*, or nobles, and the *macehualtin*, the ordinary people. Most ordinary people were farmers, who either worked their own land or the land owned by noble families. There were also the *tlacotin*, who were slaves owned by the nobles. The Valley of Mexico had excellent farming land but Aztec farmers also created 'floating islands' of heaped-up mud. The most important crops were maize, squash, sweet potato, avocado and tomato.

TENOCHTITLÁN

The ruins of the capital city of the Aztec Empire, which was home to over 200,000 people, lie under the modern-day capital, Mexico City. The city was carefully laid out on a grid of streets and canals built over swampy land. The huge city was connected to the mainland by three wide highways (right).

Gulf of Mexico

Tenochtitlán

Pacific Ocean

Tenochtitlán

Dyke

Causeway

INVASION FROM EUROPE

The history of the Americas changed when Europeans crossed the Atlantic Ocean and discovered new lands. The people who lived there must have regretted that they had been 'discovered' at all. Native Americans, north and south, were killed in huge numbers and were infected with diseases from Europe, such as smallpox and measles, against which they had no **immunity**. Invading armies were followed by new governors and merchants who transported back to the 'Old World' huge supplies of gold and silver. The Europeans also brought back plants and animals which are now familiar European foods — such as potatoes, marrows, peppers and turkeys.

GLOSSARY

A

Achilles: the Greek hero who led his warriors into battle at the seige of Troy. The adventures of Achilles are told in **Homer's** *Iliad*.

administrators: people who are employed to manage the business of an individual, a company or a country. Each administrator usually specializes in a different area of business.

agents: people who conduct business on behalf of others. For example, a merchant might sell his goods to an agent, and then the agent will sell the goods to another merchant, who will in turn sell them to his or her customers.

allegiance: in the past, people were expected to swear their allegiance to a king, queen or government. This means that they had to promise to be loyal to whoever was more powerful than them.

allied: individuals, governments or groups who share an agreement or treaty are allied.

amber: a fossil that comes from certain types of extinct trees. Amber is a beautiful yellowish-brown colour and is often used in jewellery-making.

amphitheatre: a large oval-shaped building which contains a central arena for gladiatorial displays. Seats are arranged in tiers around the central arena so that the spectators can see and hear everything that is happening.

aqueducts: a building, rather like a bridge, that carries water from one place to another, usually over quite large distances. Aqueducts are useful for taking water to farming land to help crops grow, and for supplying people in cities with fresh water.

Aramaeans: the people of ancient Syria were called Aramaeans. The Aramaean language was spoken throughout the Persian Empire.

archaeologist: someone who studies the past by scientifically examining the remains of the past. Archaeologists often **excavate** objects in their search for knowledge.

Assyrian: people who lived in northern Mesopotamia. The Assyrian Empire was at its height from the seventh to the eighth centuries BC and it stretched from Egypt to the Persian Gulf.

B

Baltic, the: the name given to the countries near the Baltic Sea — such as Poland, Denmark, Finland and Norway.

Barbarian: a name given by the Greeks and Romans to peoples who they thought of as uncivilized and warlike.

besiege: when hostile armies surround a town, attack it and prevent food and water from entering, they are besieging the town in order to force the inhabitants to surrender through starvation or thirst.

bust: the name of a portrait (usually sculpted) of a person's head and shoulders.

C

capitals: the name for the tops of columns of buildings.

caravans: the name given to groups of merchants in Asia and Africa who travel together across deserts with their goods carried by camels.

ceramic: fired clay, or an object made of fired clay, which is very hard.

civil servants: people who run the civil service. Many countries have a civil service. The civil service is the organization that runs the government of a country.

civil war: a war within a country between different groups of people of the same nationality.

colony: an area of land taken (often by force) from the people who live there by countries with trading or territorial empires. These countries are called colonial nations. Colonists are people who are sent from the colonial country to live in the newly-claimed land.

courier: another name for an official messenger.

cultivate: to tend the land in order to grow crops.

Cyclops: a Greek mythical giant, from a race of giants, with only one eye in the middle of his forehead.

D

death mask: a cast or sculpture of a person's face made just after they have died. Sometimes death masks are very realistic and sometimes they are just impressions of what people looked like.

dammed: when a barrier is built across a river, the river has been dammed.

decipher: to understand what something means.

dedicated: something (like a temple) that is devoted to one particular person or God.

dialect: a variation of a language that is spoken in one particular area of a country.

Dynasty: the name given to a family or a series of related rulers in China.

E

Edo: a member of the Negro people of Benin in south-west Nigeria. These people are well-known for their sixteenth-century bronze sculptures.

elk: a large deer that lives in north America, northern Europe and Asia. In north America an elk is called a moose.

embalm: to preserve something, such as a body, by drying it and treating it with chemicals.

emigrate: to leave one's home to start a new life in another country.

enlightenment: to have seen the light or the truth about life.

epic: a very long poem which tells a story or a series of adventures. Epics were originally passed down the generations by word-of-mouth. Later, these stories were written down so that they would not be lost or forgotten.

excavated: to find and dig up an item from the past is to excavate it. Bones, objects, and entire buildings have been excavated.

export: to sell and transport goods from one country to another.

F

fermented: a chemical reaction in a food or drink usually caused by yeast. This chemical reaction turns sugar into alcohol.

fertile: lands that are capable of growing many crops or people who are capable of having many children are fertile.

fibre: a very thin thread of material or plant which can be spun or twisted with other fibres to make cloth, rope or a structure.

flax: a plant with blue flowers which is grown for its seeds and the **fibres** of its stem. Its stem **fibres** can be woven into cloth.

fortified: a house, town or city which is defended by either walls, watchtowers, ditches or a moat.

forum, the: the main meeting place in towns of the Roman Empire. People met at the Forum in Rome to discuss politics and conduct business.

G

gazelle: a small antelope found in Asia and Africa. Gazelles are usually brown.

Greek Orthodox Church: the Christian church of Greece. The Roman Catholic Church broke away from the Greek Orthodox Church in AD 1054.

H

hectare: the name given to an area of 10,000 square metres.

Herodotus: (c. 484–424) a Greek historian who wrote about many aspects of Greek life including nine books about the war between the Greeks and the Persians from 490–449 BC.

Homer: (c. eighth century BC) the Greek poet who wrote *The Iliad* and *The Odyssey*. These are **epic** stories of the war between the Greeks and the Trojans in the twelfth century BC. Very little is known about Homer but it is thought that he was blind.

hunter-gatherers: people who hunt and gather food in order to survive rather than cultivate land or breed animals.

I

immunity: human beings have immunity to certain illnesses, such as the common cold. This means that our bodies can resist disease and recover from illness.

immigrants: people who move to live an a country different from their place of birth are called immigrants.

import: to buy and transport goods produced in another country.

inscriptions: words, pictures or symbols carved into rock, bone, stone or wood.

intestines: the tube inside the human body which connects the stomach to the anus.

irrigate: to water farm land by a system of small canals or ditches which carry water to the fields from a source such as a river.

J

jade: a semiprecious stone used in jewellery-making. Jade can be white or green in colour.

Jebusite: a tribe in Israel who occupied Jerusalem before David captured it in 1000 BC.

K

Kushan Empire: an empire in northern India which ranged from the mouth of the River Indus to the Caspian Sea and was established in c. AD 60.

L

labyrinth: a massive series of interconnecting tunnels, usually under the ground.

lacquer: a hard, black or transparent, glossy coating made from resins found in certain trees.

Latin: the language of ancient Rome and the Roman Empire. Latin was used as the language of learning in medieval Europe. Books such as the Old and New *Testaments* of the *Bible* were written in Latin. Latin is no longer spoken anywhere so it is called a 'dead' language.

lime: a mineral found in certain types of clay.

litter: a form of transport consisting of a chair or a small bed fixed to two poles or sticks, carried from place to place.

M

mace: a weapon, rather like a club, usually held as a symbol of authority.

maize: a grain crop from Latin America which was vital to ancient Mesoamerican civilizations. Maize is sometimes called sweetcorn in Europe.

meditating: the process of thinking very deeply about a subject, usually a religious one.

mercenary: a soldier who fights for any cause or any country as long as he or she is paid.

Mesoamerica: a name for ancient central America.

migrate: to travel from one place to another in search of a home.

millet: a grain crop grown to feed animals such as cows.

Minos: the legendary king of the Minoans who ruled Crete for nine years and talked with the king of the gods, Zeus.

missionary: someone who tries to convert people from one religion to another.

Moses: the leader of the Israelites in the *Old Testament* of the *Bible*. Moses led the Israelites out of slavery in Egypt and brought them to the Promised Land. God spoke to Moses and, through him, gave the Israelites their religious laws.

N

nomadic: people who travel from place to place in search of food for themselves and their cattle.

nutrients: minerals absorbed by the roots of plants as foods which help growth.

O

oases: **fertile** places in deserts where water can be found.

Odysseus: the hero of **Homer's** *Iliad*. Odysseus fought at the seige of Troy. *The Iliad* is the story of his many adventures on his journey home from war.

Ostrogoths: the name of the eastern Goths who ruled their own Italian empire.

Ottoman Turks: the Turkish people whose empire stretched through Asia, Africa and Europe. The Ottoman Turks began their invasion of the Near East in the thirteenth century.

P

palm oil: oil taken from palm trees and used in cooking.

pasture: fields set aside for animals to graze on.

pith: the area between the rind or covering of a fruit or plant and the fruit itself.

Pliny: (c. AD 23–79) a Roman scientist and historian who also wrote about geography and the natural world. Pliny was killed in the eruption of Mount Vesuvius (see page 45).

prophet: a person whom a god speaks through, or someone who communicates knowledge about a religion to its followers.

R

reservoirs: constructed lakes that are built to ensure a steady water supply for people. Reservoirs are usually made by **damming** a river.

ritual: a series of actions usually associated with a religious ceremony.

S

sacred: an object or building that is **dedicated** to one particular God, or an object or place that is thought of as holy because of its connection with a religion or a god.

Sassanian Empire: this empire stretched over parts of India and the Near East around the Persian Gulf. The Sassanians took over the Parthian Empire in the third century AD.

scarab beetle: a type of bettle used to represent the Egyptian sun god. The ancient Egyptians thought that the scarab beetle was **sacred**.

scholars: people whose life work is to study. Scholars can become experts in many, or one particular subject.

Seven Wonders of the Ancient World: the seven man-made monuments thought to be the 'wonders of the world' by ancient and medieval **scholars**. The seven wonders were the pyramids of Egypt (see pages 27, 28 and 29), the Hanging Gardens of Babylon (see page 20), the statue of Zeus at Olympia (see page 38), the Temple of Artemis at Ephesus (see page 45), the tomb of Halicarnassus, the Colossus of Rhodes and the lighthouse of Alexandria.

Shona: the name of the language and the people of modern-day Zimbabwe and Mozambique.

Sogdian: people of ancient central Asia who lived in the kingdom of Sogdiana. Their capital city was Samarkand.

subcontinent: a large identifiable area of land within a continent.

suckled: to be fed with milk from a female animal.

survey: to study land or people in great detail.

T

tributaries: a body of water, such as a stream or a river that joins up with a larger river.

V

Valley of the Kings: the burial grounds of the Egyptian kings (pharaohs). The Valley of the Kings is opposite the ancient city of Thebes on the River Nile in Upper Egypt.

variegated: something which has had colours added to it or which has a pattern which gives the impression of constantly changing its appearance.

Y

Yoruba: people from west Africa, mainly from the coast of north-west Nigeria. The Yoruba lived in city-states and made beautiful art and music.

INDEX

Major topics (ones which have chapter headings or are in lists of page numbers) appear in **bold**.